CHURCH AND GNOSIS

AMS PRESS
NEW YORK

CHURCH & GNOSIS

A study of
Christian thought and speculation
in the Second Century

THE MORSE LECTURES FOR 1931

BY

F. C. BURKITT, D.D.

Hon. D.Litt. (Durham)

CAMBRIDGE
AT THE UNIVERSITY PRESS
1932

Library of Congress Cataloging in Publication Data

Burkitt, Francis Crawford, 1864-1935.
    Church & gnosis.

    Reprint of the 1932 ed. published by the University
Press, Cambridge, which was the Morse lecture for 1931.
    Includes index.
    1. Gnosticism. 2. Theology, Doctrinial—History—
Early church, ca. 30-600. I. Title. II. Series:
The Morse lectures; 1931.
BT1390.B83   1978   230'.1'3   77-84696
ISBN 0-404-16104-9

From the edition of 1932, Cambridge
First AMS edition published in 1978

Manufactured in the United States of America

AMS PRESS, INC.
NEW YORK, N.Y.

TO

PRESIDENT HENRY S. COFFIN
AND THE PROFESSORS OF
UNION THEOLOGICAL SEMINARY
NEW YORK

I DEDICATE THIS BOOK
IN REMEMBRANCE OF THE DELIGHTFUL
KINDNESS AND HOSPITALITY SHEWN
TO MY WIFE AND MYSELF
DURING OUR STAY AMONG THEM IN
OCTOBER, 1931

PREFACE

THE five Lectures in this volume were delivered in October 1931 at Union Theological Seminary, New York, as the Morse Lectures for that year. The question with which they deal is not so remote from present-day problems as might appear at first sight. From one point of view the problem which beset the Christian thinker of the second century is similar to that which confronts us now, how to express in terms appropriate to our modern world the Gospel Message that was proclaimed in a society so far away from us and so different in outlook. And doubtless it is not only a question of words and names, of mere appropriateness of terms, that confronts us. Our world, our conception of the world, is different from the horizon of Galilee and Judaea in the days of Jesus. How are we to conserve the value of the 'treasure', seeing that the 'earthen vessels' in which it was first stored are so unsuitable, and in some cases worn out and broken by the lapse of time? This also was the problem before the men of the second century, when the Gospel had been transferred from Pales-

tine to Europe and from a Semitic environment
into the cultivated, scientific, philosophical civilization of the Graeco-Roman world.

The Graeco-Roman world has passed away. Its
philosophy and its science is antiquated, mere
milestones on the road by which man has reached
his present outlook, an outlook vaster, stranger,
mistier, yet we believe truer than ever before
attained. But at the time the claims of that philosophy and science were as imperious as those of
our modern astronomy, biology, economics are
to us. Anything that claimed to be true religion
had to take account of that philosophy and science.
It seemed to me, therefore, not uninteresting to
consider in detail some of the efforts of second-
century Christians to effect a synthesis, even if they
serve as much as a warning as an encouragement.

In a certain sense, of course, this little book is
controversial. A main thesis has been to up-
hold the old-fashioned view that 'the Gnostics'
were Christians, heretics no doubt, but Christian
heretics, rather than pagans with a few Christian
traits. To the Gnostics, as I view them, the Figure
of Jesus the Saviour was central, and their intention was not so much syncretistic, as an effort to
represent Jesus and the 'salvation' which He
brought in an aspect suitable for the acceptance
of educated and cultivated men and women. The

PREFACE

culture and education of that day is alien to us, but that only teaches us that the effort made by the Gnostics is an effort we also should make. The goal is not a static perfection of statement, which (if achieved) would only mean ossification. What is necessary is the effort to express in our own tongues the *magnalia Dei*, in language that really means something to us, though it may be different from the hallowed syllables of antiquity.

F. C. BURKITT

CAMBRIDGE

February 1932

NOTE

The founder of the Morse Lectures
was the celebrated artist and pioneer
in telegraphy. In his honour I composed the Border round the Title-page
of this book. I suppose that every
Boy Scout or Girl Guide who reads
this book can make it out, but for
the benefit of others it is here transcribed.

Top

MORSE LECTURES

Left side, down

UNION THEOL. SEMINARY

Bottom

NEW YORK

Right side, up

ANNO DOMINI 1931

CONTENTS

'However much obscurity surrounds the rise of Gnosticism, the one thing that is certain is that Christian-Hellenistic Gnosis arose out of Christian Eschatological Gnosis.'

A. Schweitzer, *The Mysticism of S. Paul*, p. 74.

'He who possesses a heart that is sanctified, and that shines with light, is blest with the vision of God.'

Fragment of Valentinus, quoted by E. F. Scott (*ERE* VI 231) from Clement of Alexandria.

Chapter I

INTRODUCTION

They thought that the Kingdom of God should immediately appear.
Lk. xix 11.

AMONG the subjects suggested to me by friends as appropriate for this series of Lectures was the connexion between the Gospel according to S. John and the religion of the Mandaeans. I did not accept the suggestion for my main subject, because I felt that a full treatment of this question would be somewhat too technical and detailed, though I hope to touch upon it in the course of what I have to say. But the fact that the suggestion was made may be used to explain my actual choice of subject and what I mean by it.

It is a paradox that there should be learned men who do actually hold that any significant connexion should exist between the Fourth Gospel and Mandaean documents. The Fourth Gospel was written at the end of the first century of our era, or at latest very early in the second century; it has been canonical Scripture among Christians for some eighteen and a half centuries. The Mandaeans, who still exist on the lower reaches of the Tigris and the Euphrates, profess a peculiar religion, neither

Christian nor Jewish, though not altogether disconnected with these; their sacred writings were not collected together into their present form before the middle of the seventh century A.D. In some of these writings John the Baptist is particularly honoured, and a paradoxical theory has been started, supported by some distinguished German theologians, that these Mandaeans are partly derived from non-Christian followers of John the Baptist. What is still more paradoxical, it has actually been held that our Gospel 'of John' is only a Christianized rewriting of an original Gospel of John the Baptist, which had the Baptist and not Jesus Christ for its Hero. 'There was a man sent from God whose name was John'—this is the first statement made in the Fourth Gospel when it descends to earth and comes to speak of the world of men: it has been suggested that in the original form it was John, and not Jesus, who was set forth as the Word of GOD!

It is a paradox that such a view should have been put forward, and I for one do not believe that there is any truth in the view. But that the view should have been held at all by responsible and learned investigators of early Christianity is both significant and instructive. It shews us that these learned men feel that there is something odd and strange in the development of the Christian Religion and the Christian Church, that the actual history of the Christian Church does not seem to them to be naturally illustrated by the surviving documents.

The documents themselves seem to be in need of fresh explanation. The Catholic Church, as it actually took shape during the second century, does not, to many people, seem naturally to grow out of the original Gospel. There is a gap, a discontinuity, somewhere; where are we to place it, and what is its nature? This is the great question in the study of the rise of Christianity. That eccentricities, such as the attempted correlation of the Fourth Gospel with Mandaean doctrines, can still find favour, seems to me to shew that no satisfactory answer to the great question has yet been generally arrived at.

Any elementary text-book of Church History will tell us that the special preoccupation of Church thinkers during the second century was the struggle with 'Gnostic' heresies, in the course of which a firmer and clearer orthodox presentation of Christianity emerged. Mandaean ideas have undoubtedly a certain kinship with some Gnostic ideas; the Fourth Gospel has always hitherto been regarded as a mine of orthodox Church doctrine. It has seemed to me therefore that a general consideration of some of the main problems that exercised Christian thought in the second century will be the most suitable way of considering both the ideas of the Fourth Gospel and those of the Mandaeans. The title 'Church and Gnosis' includes this special question under a more general heading.

3

GNOSIS

Before considering any particular Gnostic theory, or describing what Christians had believed before the Gnostics appeared on the scene, it will be well to define what we mean by Gnosis. 'Gnosis' sounds very much more formidable and technical in English or German than it does in Greek. γνῶσισ is 'knowledge'. The word occurs in the Old and the New Testaments in all sorts of connotations, good and bad; as the Bible is so predominantly occupied with religion it is not surprising that γνῶσισ is mostly used of religious knowledge. Timothy is warned against the vain babblings of the knowledge falsely so called (1 Tim. vi 20): in the Greek it is 'the pseudonymous Gnosis' (τῆσ ψευδωνύμου γνώσεωσ). Many scholars have seen in this a direct reference to forms of what we call Gnostic heresy, but be that as it may we should remember that the phrase is not so technical in Greek as it sounds to us. In any case the familiar words of the *Benedictus* tell us that John the Baptist was to give gnosis of salvation to GOD's people (γνῶσιν σωτηρίασ, Lk. i 77). And if indeed we are to find a Scripture phrase for what the Gnostics professed to give, we cannot do better than 2 Tim. iii 15, teaching 'to make thee wise unto salvation'. What Timothy had was holy writings, i.e. the Old Testament: the Gnostics had other lore, but the idea of its value to the believer was the same.

If we go on to ask on what authority the Gnostic

4

teachers based their doctrines, it is not very easy to give an answer. A great deal of pains has been taken by modern scholars to correlate the ideas of the various teachers with this or that feature of ancient Greek or Egyptian or Iranian religion. The Christian Fathers are never tired of asking where Valentinus or Basilides got their ideas from, and on what authority they teach their doctrines. I do not suppose that the disciples of Valentinus or Basilides asked such questions. *Ipse dixit*, they said; our Master taught so-and-so. They believed in Valentinus, or whoever it may have been.

Gnosis is based, therefore, on two main factors. One is the personal authority of the teacher; the other is, indeed must be, the self-consistency of the new teaching. 'It is a poor hypothesis', said someone once, 'which does not explain more than the set of conditions for which it was originally invented.' An hypothesis which really is based on a more or less sound knowledge of the constitution of the world and the nature of man will commend itself for a considerable time. The length of the solar year is about 365 days: a year of 365 days will remain approximately correct by the sun for very much longer than a year of 360 days; and as the true length is very nearly $365\frac{1}{4}$ days, a year of 365 days with every fourth year lengthened to 366 days can be accepted as truth for centuries before the error is apparent. So the Gnostic systems which we are to examine claimed not only to be true knowledge in themselves but also to explain other mysteries. In the words of Bishop Christopher Wordsworth's well-known hymn the Gnostic feels that he can

> all truth and knowledge see
> In the beatific vision of the blessed Trinity.[1]

For the Gnostic of the second century it was not the doctrine of the Trinity, but of the Divine Pleroma or of the First Mystery taught in *Pistis Sophia*. But the principle is the same: the knowledge of the true nature of Divine things seems to the initiate to light everything up and make everything clear.

This mention of the orthodox, Catholic, doctrine of the Trinity may serve to remind us that the Gnostic method of teaching is not so unfamiliar, strange as the contents of some of the Gnostic systems may sound. At a later period Mani, the founder of the Manichaean Religion, taught in the same way, and he is rightly to be considered as a Gnostic. The Church writers preferred on the whole to trust to the tradition preserved in 'Holy Scriptures',[2] but when we examine these we find that they are themselves examples of the Gnostic method. 'Thus saith the LORD' say the Prophets: in what does this essentially differ from the *Ipse dixit* of Pythagoras? Nay more, the 'Amen, I say unto you', of Jesus is essentially the Gnostic way of teaching. And we cannot stop even here.

---

[1] 'Hark! the sound of holy voices' (*E. Hymnal* 198).
[2] ἱερὰ γράμματα, 2 Tim. iii 15.

Thales, Heraclitus, Empedocles, all the great Ionian Greeks, taught like the almost mythical Pythagoras a Gnosis.

Was there any exception in antiquity? Yes, there was one great exception, one pioneer of a new way of teaching, a man who disclaimed to have any special Gnosis or Wisdom. He was, he said, no teacher of Wisdom but only a lover of Wisdom, a 'philo-sopher'. Socrates believed that Truth was self-evident to every sane and unprejudiced man. The trouble was that men were full of prejudices, which obstructed true notions from coming out from the depths of their consciences into the open: his business was that of a midwife, to help men to bring their true notions to the birth by removing the obstructions. This was a new thing in the world, a new way of regarding Truth altogether, which has not yet reached its final concordat with what may be summed up as Sacred Tradition.

The 'maieutic' method of Socrates had an immense influence on civilized thought, but there is very little of it in our second-century Gnostics. They are, we may say, like Ionian seers and speculators born out of due time. It must be clearly remembered that the Gnostics come before us historically as Christians. The victorious school of Church writers regarded Valentinus and the other 'Gnostic' thinkers as heretics, and such they were. They set forth views about the manifestation of Jesus in the world and the salvation for men to be obtained through Him, which were different from those of the main body of Christians. In many ways the judgement of history supports the Catholic writers, such as Irenaeus: much of the Gnostic teaching was fantastic and in direct opposition to fact. But Valentinus and his fellows started from Christian ideas, they were attempting to formulate a Christian theory of GOD and man; the contest between Catholics and Gnostics was a struggle between persons who felt themselves to be Christians, not between Christians and heathens.

We are accustomed to think of orthodox Christianity as a more or less definite system. Perhaps we may not quite accept it for ourselves, but at least we are conscious of the standard by which we can measure our own unorthodoxy or heterodoxy. Christianity, we feel, *is* that which is set forth in the Thirty-nine Articles, or the Shorter Catechism, or the *Summa* of S. Thomas Aquinas. After all, these venerable documents do agree a good deal together; a set of statements embodying the points in which these essentially agree would make a theological document of respectable length. Romans, Anglicans and Presbyterians might each severally say that very important points had been passed over or inadequately set forth, but so far as the document went it would express their view of Christian doctrine. But though it might, on careful examination, be approved by Irenaeus and Tertullian, I do not think it would sound familiar to them. Christian doctrine during the second century was still in a process of formulation. The great Gnostic thinkers were Heretics, not in the sense that they left the high road, but in the sense that the track along which they went was not the direction along which the high road was afterwards constructed.

I have said that the Gnostics come before us historically as Christians. This is the traditional view, but it is not the view which has been current in quite modern times. The view which has found a great deal of favour in recent years is to regard 'the Gnosis' as a kind of philosophy derived from the Orient, from that East which was only superficially influenced by Greek thought and clarity, a philosophy which is supposed to have been current in the eastern parts of the Roman Empire during the centuries that followed Alexander the Great, and particularly during the first two centuries of our era. This view has been upheld with great learning by such scholars as Bousset and Reitzenstein; if I take the other side it is not only because I think the several systems are best understood when considered as Christian systems, however aberrant, but because I wish above all to point out that the dominant cause, the moving factor which led to the excogitation of these systems, was something inherent in Christianity and the beliefs of the earliest Christians. We come back to the gap or discontinuity or crisis in Christian thought of which I have already spoken, which I have called the great question in the study of the rise of Christianity. The view I am going to put before you in these Lectures is that the prime factor in the rise of the Gnostic systems is connected with what is commonly now called Eschatology, that is to say, the problem raised for the Christian Church by the non-arrival of the Last Day and of the confidently expected Second Coming of Christ.

PRIMITIVE CHRISTIAN BELIEFS

Primitive Christian Beliefs are nowhere summed up better than in the familiar words of the First Epistle to the Thessalonians: 'Ye turned to GOD from idols to serve a living and true GOD, and to wait for His Son from heaven whom He raised from the dead—Jesus who delivers us from the wrath to come' (i 9, 10). To wait for Jesus; and, as you know, the converted Thessalonians expected Jesus to come so soon, that they had to be warned not to leave off working altogether, and to be told that of the actual time and season of the Coming no one knew.

Scholars have come to realize for themselves that the Thessalonians had more excuse for their mistaken way of life than was formerly taught. If what is called the Eschatological view of early Christianity has made great progress during the present century it is not due merely to the eloquence and brilliance of such writers as Johannes Weiss and Albert Schweitzer. They did not invent the so-called Eschatological view: what they did was to allow the New Testament to speak for itself. 'The Kingdom of GOD is at hand', said Jesus. The Good

News, the Gospel, was that it was at hand. We read in the tradition that various counsels were given by Jesus to His 'apostles', His missionaries—what they were to take, or not take, for their journeys, how they were to behave in towns and villages friendly and unfriendly, how they were to endure opposition, persecution, and even imprisonment. It is often supposed by critics that some of these directions and anticipations—those, for example, which speak of standing before kings and governors and of being a testimony to all the nations— reflect the experiences of later times. It may indeed be so, but the message these missionaries are told to deliver remains unexpanded. It is still that the Kingdom of G O D is at hand and therefore that men should repent,—that, and no more![1]

The Kingdom of G O D did not arrive, and the missionaries returned before the Son of Man had come. Jesus, if we may follow the indications given us by Mark, spent the summer and autumn after His first public activity in semi-retirement to the north and east of the Holy Land. When He comes forward again it is what Wellhausen so finely called 'a transfigured Jesus',[2] who is determined to go up to Jerusalem on a forlorn hope, ready to give His life as a ransom for many. When He arrives in Jerusalem He does do something public in the Temple Courts, and with some success and public favour. But the heavens do not

[1] Matt. x 7, Lk. x 9, 11; Mk. vi 12.
[2] Wellhausen, *Das Evangelium Marci* (1909), p. 62.

move; neither from heaven nor from men is the response at all of a kind which gives Him, Jesus, assurance of support, and—here again I am following what Mark tells us—He gives up all worldly hope. He does not abandon His claims to authority, but He deliberately dashes the enthusiasm of the crowds by telling those who ask Him about tribute to give Caesar his due, and He leaves the Temple, never to return. And, according to Mark, He then not only anticipates His own immediate death (Mk. xiv 8), but also warns His intimate friends not to be too hasty and eager in expecting the Coming of the Son of Man (Mk. xiii 5-37).

In this famous 'eschatological' discourse, what is really remarkable is not the prediction that the Son of Man would come, but the warning that there may be a painful delay. The great Day will be in that generation indeed, but not yet. Much has yet to happen, there is even danger that the disciples may forget it and be caught unawares. This is a new note in the Gospel story. As it comes in Mark, it sounds to me genuine, words in their historical setting, the voice of one who had learned, not from holy oracles but from bitter experience, that the End would not be yet.

Then came the tragedy of Good Friday; but it was followed by the conviction of Peter and those who joined Peter that the Master had risen from the dead and would soon, very soon, come again in glory as the Messiah, as the Son of Man coming

with the clouds and all the holy angels with Him
to inaugurate the Kingdom of GOD. In these
terms the Gospel was reformulated. In the words
that I have already quoted from the First Epistle to
the Thessalonians the believers were to wait for
GOD's Son from heaven, even Jesus who would be
their deliverer from the wrath to come.

When would He come?

They thought, says a passage in the Gospel, that
the Kingdom of GOD should immediately appear.
This passage (Lk. xix 11) might very well stand as
a motto for the whole of the New Testament. Even
the writer of the First Epistle of John warns those
to whom he speaks that it was then 'the last hour'.

PAUL

In sketching the development of thought within
the Christian community, however hastily and
sketchily, it is necessary to take each leader of
thought separately. It is in individuals, not in
societies, that thought progresses, and the thought
of great men outruns that of their contemporaries.
It is true that later disciples may imitate the works
of original leaders of thought, but such composi-
tions re-echo rather than produce new tones, or
else they are different altogether. To come to the
concrete instances to which these general remarks
are meant to apply, I find it difficult to believe that
the Epistles to the Philippians, Colossians, Ephesians were written by a school of followers and
imitators of S. Paul, of whom we otherwise know

nothing. They are not centos of Pauline phrases, nor mere echoes of his earlier teaching, but press forward into new problems with true Pauline daring and insight, yet with enough marks of Pauline style, both in language and sentiment, to justify the traditional ascription to the great Apostle of the Gentiles. The Pastoral Epistles, on the other hand, seem to me in a different category. Not only are the linguistic marks of Pauline authorship absent, but the stress laid on the deposit (1 Tim. vi 20)[1] is not characteristic of the pioneer but of the man of the second generation.

In the matter of the Second Coming, of Eschatology and all the problems connected with it, I feel most strongly that Paul was a pioneer, and a lonely pioneer. He began, like all the early Christians, with an expectation of the Parusia of Christ in the immediate future. This is obvious from 1 Cor. xv 50 ff., whichever readings we adopt as correct. The matter is even clearer in 1 Thess. iv 17 ('we the living who survive'), but this very definite phraseology may come not so much from Paul himself as from Silvanus, i.e. Silas the Jerusalemite,[2] whom I regard as the actual writer of the Thessalonian Letters. Still in any case it was approved by S. Paul, and indeed no one doubts that he, like the other early believers, was expecting the End in that generation. It is surely the expectation

[1] And, I would add, the new *birth* (Tit. iii 5).
[2] Acts xv 22 (ἐξ αὐτῶν): see my *Christian Beginnings*, pp. 128–33.

of a speedy consummation of all human affairs
rather than an ascetic theory of morals that makes
Paul discourage his Corinthian friends from marriage. It is because of the present unfavourable
state of things (1 Cor. vii 26). What indeed is
implied, both there and in the whole New Testament, is that a man may marry and have children,
but hardly grandchildren. The notion that there
may be successive generations of Christians, and
that one of the most solemn duties of a God-
fearing man is to do the best for those that shall
come after him, is conspicuous by its absence. In
its place we find 'Be not anxious for the morrow'.

But the thought of the coming Parusia did not
fill S. Paul's mind at any time. He was more
occupied with GOD's plan of salvation. A most
important part of this, according to his view, lay
already in the Past. The disciples of Jesus had
confidence in their Master. They became convinced that He was GOD's chosen Messiah, and
they expected His speedy return to set all wrongs
right. Such an attitude of mind can be called
Faith: it might equally well be called Hope. Either
word not unfairly sums up their general attitude.
This is the religious theory expressed in the early
chapters of Acts. Herod and Pontius Pilate may
have conspired 'against the LORD and His Christ',
but it had been all foretold and the evil deed had
been overruled for good.

S. Paul had, as we all know, a more profound
view of the significance of the career of Jesus and

His Crucifixion. The 'word of the Cross' that Paul proclaimed was more than the tale of a tragic crime. Christ had died for us; through the Crucifixion we had somehow been bought with a price away from the dominion of evil, even though at the time we were still sinners, and the experience of Christ's death we must sacramentally—that is, really but not sensibly—undergo when we join the Christian Society. I need not further elaborate the Pauline doctrine, so familiar to all of us. But we may notice that the acceptance of these ideas, which S. Paul calls Faith, refers to the Past. It is distinct from the common Christian belief in and expectation of the Parusia. Paul therefore had need of two words: there was *Faith* which refers to the Past, and *Hope* which refers to the Future. Moreover there was another element. It was not enough, according to S. Paul, to believe in the redemption from evil accomplished by the Cross and all that the Cross signified, and further to look forward to an ultimate attainment of a Kingdom of GOD which was not eating and drinking but righteousness and peace and joy in holy spirit. More was required: the Christian was required not only to believe in this and to hope for this, but also to like it. GOD loves a cheerful giver, and also a cheerful receiver of His inestimable benefits: this temper of mind is *Charity*. I feel convinced that the *Agape* described in 1 Cor. xiii is neither philanthropy nor enthusiastic devotion, but the attitude towards GOD which Paul exemplifies when he says 'Thanks be to GOD for His unspeakable gift!' (2 Cor. ix 15).

Thus the major part, one might say two-thirds, of S. Paul's religion was not concentrated on the Christian Hope of the Coming of Christ, even when his hope of its speedy fulfilment was most vivid. Meanwhile time went on and Paul found himself getting on in years, faced moreover with the prospect of death at the hands of the civil power if not from old age. Young converts like Timothy were now in the prime of life, men whose whole active career had been passed in the Christian Society, in Christian conditions; indeed there must have been not a few children, born of Christian parents, who had been brought up in the Faith, who had been received into the Church, and had died. Yet the Lord had not yet come.

The conclusion which S. Paul drew was that the Church in itself must be of more significance than was at first realized. It was itself an important thing in GOD's sight, and therefore something eternal.

It is in the circular letter which we call the Epistle to the Ephesians that this view of the Church is most clearly set forth, but the doctrine that the Church is the body of the Christ is clearly laid down in Colossians (i 18, 24), including the very remarkable idea that the sufferings of himself, Paul, and therefore of other faithful Christians, are a sort of required supplement (ὑστέρημα) to Christ's own sufferings. The doctrine taught in Ephesians is only an amplification of this, and I for one regard Ephesians as the genuine work of Paul himself.

We are so accustomed to the familiar phrases of Ephesians and Colossians that we hardly see what a revolution in Christian thought they represent. Or rather we ought to say that they represent a development of Christian ideas, that opened out a passage along which Christian thought could travel when the old avenue of the hope of a speedy arrival of the End was beginning to close up.

The Thessalonian believers had acted consistently with their beliefs. They had been content to 'wait for Jesus' and to take no thought for the morrow. Why should they? The things of this world, as they believed, were transitory and worthless.

> Cur mundus militat sub uana gloria
> cuius prosperitas est transitoria?
> tam cito labitur eius potentia
> quam uasa figuli que sunt fragilia.

The practical instinct of Paul would have none of this line of conduct, though I do not find that he and Silas had yet found a satisfactory theoretical critique of the Thessalonians' *konsequente Eschatologie*. But after some ten or twelve years more of varied Christian experience, with the End of all earthly things not yet come and his own death in sight, he found his new theory of the place of the Church, here and now, in the scheme of things.

Unlike a large number of critical scholars, I believe (as I said just now) in the Pauline authorship of the Epistle to the Ephesians. The main weight

18

of the objections to the Pauline authorship I think is not linguistic, as is the case with the Pastoral Epistles, but the difficulty of fitting the ideas of the Ephesian Epistle into 'Paulinism'. The Paulinism expounded by theologians has for its basal axiom the notion that Paul had a closed system of thought, the same or nearly the same from soon after his conversion to the day of his death. This seems to me highly improbable. I think Paul was much influenced both by the mere lapse of time and by the greatness of his own work. In one case we know of a change: in 1 Corinthians he was expecting to be alive at the Parusia (1 Cor. xv 51), in Philippians he calmly contemplates his probable death. I cannot but think that Paul's active mind must in any case, apart from the evidence offered by Ephesians, have considered what was the significance of this present time, when the Christian Society was ever growing and developing, and nevertheless the End was not yet come.

My main theme is the Gnostics and their Gnosis, and I do not want to delay too long on the familiar ground of Pauline ideas. They are familiar to us, because they are included in the New Testament, but at the time of writing 'Ephesians' had no such authority. So far as we can judge from the evidence, the letter—a circular one, not a mere local missive —made a good impression, and it appears never to have been quite forgotten. The general conclusion to be drawn from the admirable tables at the end of the book compiled by the Oxford Society of

Historical Theology on the 'Apostolic Fathers'[1] is that the writings of Paul which remained in circulation during the fifty years or so which followed his death were 1 Corinthians, Romans, and Ephesians. The evidence is consistent with the theory that makes the resuscitation of the others, notably 2 Corinthians and Galatians, to be due to the energy of Marcion, but it is evident that our 'First Epistle to the Corinthians' with 'Romans' and 'Ephesians' had never dropped out of memory.

But this did not mean more than that they were honoured writings of a great Missionary, to be studied and imitated, and here and there (where the application was obvious) to be quoted (Clement xlvii 1 = 1 Cor. i 11 ff.). The influence of Paul as a Doctor of the Church came later, and none of the Apostolic Fathers is a Paulinist in the sort of way that S. Augustine or Luther or Pascal may be called Paulinists.

As I view the matter, the age of looking back, of appeal to the pure beliefs of 'primitive' times, had not yet arrived. It was a time of the rapid development of new customs, new organization, ideas new to some extent, at least. The Church, the Christian Society, was rapidly becoming an almost exclusively Greek-speaking body. Latin Christianity was hardly yet in existence, and the Destruction of Jerusalem in A.D. 70 had shattered for ever the con-

[1] *The New Testament in the Apostolic Fathers* (Oxford, 1905), pp. 137 f.

trolling influence of Jerusalemite and Judaistic Christianity, as a living active force. Judaic influence in the future would be a literary force, derived from the Old Testament as understood by Christian Greeks.

And meanwhile the old 'eschatological' view of the world and its fate continued to persist in almost unabated strength. Indeed the Jewish War and the collapse of the Jewish State must have helped to keep it alive both among Jews, as witnessed by 4 Ezra and the Apocalypse of Baruch, and also among Christians, as witnessed by the Revelation of John and the Ascension of Isaiah. Beliefs, such as the return of Nero from the East and the advent of fresh world-wide calamities ushering in the End, were current and have laid their mark on contemporary literature. Yet still the End did not come. The world went jolting along its accustomed course; in fact, with the second century of our era there arrived that prosperous period of Roman history when Trajan and his successors were on the throne and civilization, Graeco-Roman civilization, seemed to be established firmer than ever. Could the Christian theory of the world stand the strain of an age of prosperity? The Church still continued to increase, but did it teach a theory, a theology, fit for an enlightened, educated man? Was there not a call for a new theology, something which would explain the true nature of the 'Salvation' attained mysteriously by Christians in terms of current 'enlightened' ideas? Could not this ordinary

Christianity be more properly expressed in terms which cultured people could use? Was not such a cultured expression more near to absolute truth than the vulgar enunciation of the new Religion that was sufficient for the uneducated common folk? It was only natural that such questions should begin to be asked: in due time they gave rise to such 'Gnostic' systems as those of Valentinus and Basilides. Meanwhile there was an even more pressing theological problem for Churchmen. They had to make up their minds how they were to regard the Old Testament.

THE PROBLEM OF THE OLD TESTAMENT

It is easy to forget that the Old Testament and its significance was to the second generation of Christians very much of a problem. They came in the end to conclusions which seemed so satisfactory that it has been only in our day, in the light of the new knowledge derived from science and historical criticism, that they have been disturbed and new problems have arisen. What I mean can best be understood from a consideration of the long-lost work of S. Irenaeus known as the *Epideixis*, happily now found to be extant in an Armenian translation and published in 1907.[1]

This work is by the author of the famous refutation of Gnostic heresies, a refutation which

[1] *Des hl. Irenäus Schrift*...εἰς ἐπίδειξιν...herausgegeben von Dr Karapet Ter-Mekerttschian (T. und U. xxxi, Heft 1), Leipzig, 1907.

is also the most ancient and faithful account of the chief systems that are usually reckoned as Gnostic. The *Epideixis* does not describe or refute unorthodox errors, but gives a sort of epitome of the orthodox Christian system, representing it as prepared for by the Old Dispensation of which the Old Testament is the record, the author illustrating his thesis by copious citations from the Old Testament itself. Read carefully, the peculiar tendencies of S. Irenaeus are everywhere to be seen: no one doubts the genuineness of the discovery, and specialists have given it most of the attention it deserves. But the general theological public, the sort of public that is interested in the *Didache* or the Oxyrhynchus so-called *Logia*, took very little interest in the *Epideixis*. Why? I think some of the older readers of it knew very well. They recognized in it the Bible teaching of their youth, of 'Line upon Line', of countless Scripture manuals, of the Shorter Catechism. It was a teaching which annexed the Hebrew Bible to the Christian Church, with the corollary that the meaning of that Bible was in every part the doctrine of the Church, and that those parts of the Bible that did not seem to set forth the doctrine of the Church might be practically (but not formally) ignored as being of only temporary significance. This masterful solution—both parts of it—had not been arrived at all at once. Let me hasten to add that as compared with some of the alternative theories, there is something to be said for it. We still hear from time to time in some quarters that there is too much of the Old Testament in Christianity. The best answer to this is that many scholars tend nowadays to treat Christianity as one of the pagan Mystery-Religions. If the Church had not been determined to claim the Old Testament for its own, to declare itself the true Israel and the heir of the Old Testament anticipations, I think it would have been swept away from an historical view of Religion altogether.

It is difficult to conceive historical Catholicism without the Old Testament; perhaps the best way to proceed is to consider some of the solutions of the Old Testament problem which were not adopted by the Church. First, then, let us take the Epistle of Barnabas. Here we are not far from orthodoxy: we are considering a work that at one time in some quarters found a place in the New Testament itself. We see, too, how the problem of the Old Testament tended to present itself to very ordinary minds. The difficulty was that the Old Testament plainly commanded certain things which Christians did not obey, for example, not to eat hare. This is explained by 'Barnabas' as really condemning this or that vicious practice, enforcing his exegesis with false natural history.[1] According to this view, then, the Old Testament was moral from cover to cover, but was absurdly worded. The Church had the good sense to reject this view as a whole, though retaining it in certain places. It is

[1] μὴ γένῃ, φησί, παιδοφθόροσ (*Barn*. x).

suicidal to accept a Book as sacred and at the same time to declare the natural meaning of its words not to be the meaning.[1]

Another solution, even more radical than that of 'Barnabas', is specially associated with the great heretic teacher Marcion. Marcion is commonly reckoned among the Gnostics, but I venture to think he is distinct from these and is best regarded as a separate thinker. He was impressed above all things by the newness of the religion announced by Jesus and its difference from that which had gone before. To him the God of the Old Testament was very nearly the Devil of the New. The God of the Old Testament was to Marcion a God of ruthless Justice, and no more. Marcion rejected that God, and regarded the Old Testament as the Book of this ruthless Being. The special weakness of Marcion's view of the Old Testament is that it is inconsistent with the historical Jesus, and as Marcion based his own religion upon Jesus his views about the Old Testament are a jumble of inconsistency, as the Church Fathers were not slow to point out.

But between these radical extremes there were many other theories, one of which at least is

[1] I do not mean that authors, sacred or profane, may not from time to time express themselves in a metaphorical or cryptic style, so that the real meaning may be different from what appears at first sight, but in such cases the metaphorical cryptic meaning *is* the meaning intended by the author. No one could seriously maintain this with reference to the food laws of Deuteronomy.

associated with a distinguished Gnostic teacher. The 'Letter of Ptolemaeus to Flora', preserved by Epiphanius, gives us an excellent idea of the kind of quality in the Old Testament which made it to cultivated Christians of the second century a problem and a difficulty.

The solution of Ptolemaeus is that we must distinguish various elements in the Old Testament. There is a truly Divine nucleus, but there are also inferior elements. Some things were added by Moses because of the hardness of the Israelites' hearts, and so are not part of the perfect ideal legislation. Some things were added by the Elders not by Moses, and are therefore (according to Ptolemaeus) not approved by our Saviour. Other things are truly GOD's Laws, but even here we must distinguish. The Decalogue is Divine, but 'eye for eye, tooth for tooth', is not legislation for all time: Jesus taught us to forgive our enemies, and also that GOD will forgive His penitent children. Further, there are other things, like circumcision and the sacrifices, that are typical: in themselves they are irrational, but they signified the true salvation that was to come through Jesus.

A modification of this theory is to be found in the ancient early Christian, non-Gnostic work, called the *Didascalia*. Possibly the *Didascalia* is independent altogether of Ptolemaeus, but both systems recognize a temporary element in the Law, an element which is not obligatory for Christians either to obey or to defend.

In this Introductory Lecture I have emphasized two things, the Eschatological Hope of the Second Coming of Jesus and the authority of the Old Testament. I do so, because I think that these two things were the main possessions, the visible property, the main stock-in-trade, so to speak, with which Gentile Christianity started. There was the germ of much else, some of which is of the highest importance, but these two things bulked largest. You see them put forward, with admirable historical tact, in the discourse put into the mouth of S. Paul at Athens by the writer of the Book of Acts. The first part of Paul's discourse is an attack on 'idolatry' quite in the manner of the Old Testament: this leads up to an announcement of the Last Judgement and the Parusia of Jesus (Acts xvii 30f.). To the Greek both parts were strange, foreign, uncouth, barbarous. But if he felt the power and the attraction of the new Religion he had to come to terms with both parts. They were, each of them, a challenge. When, after more than a century of thought and controversy, a 'Catholic' philosophy had grown up, a long-enduring synthesis came to be generally accepted by very nearly all who professed and called themselves Christians. But this interval, this century, is the era of the so-called 'Gnostic' teachers, of Valentinus, of Basilides, and many another. It seems to me that the first condition of rightly regarding them is to consider them as Christians who were striving to set forth the living essence of their Religion in a form uncontaminated by the Jewish envelope in which they had received it, and expressed in terms more suited (as they might say) to the cosmogony and philosophy of their enlightened age.

Chapter II

PHILOSOPHICAL GNOSTICISM

IN the previous introductory chapter I have attempted to sketch the salient characteristics of the earliest Christianity, as they might be expected to strike a Gentile inquirer. He would find a belief that the God or Cult-Hero worshipped by the Christians had appeared in Judaea a generation or two ago, and that He was expected soon to come again in glory; and he also would find that the Christians reverenced a Sacred Book, viz. what we call the Old Testament.

We may now go on to consider some of the ideas or prejudices which it would be likely for this inquirer himself to hold. Some features of resemblance are to be found in certain very widely separated 'Gnostic' systems. They must have a common origin, but I venture to think that the common origin is to be found in certain widely spread notions or ideas rather than in particular systems of religion or philosophy.

ASTROLOGY

First of all we have to consider the ideas that are grouped round the word Astrology. In our days 'Astrology' means the traditional pseudo-science of the influence of the stars, in contrast to the real science of 'Astronomy', based on continual fresh observation and on hypotheses which are made to conform to the results of observation. Astronomers have excogitated the Solar System, not because they like it or because it ministers to human vanity, but because that arrangement of things alone accounts for the actual observed positions of sun, moon, and stars. But in the first and second centuries of our era what we now call astrology represented a real advance of scientific theory over ancient tradition. Astrology is bound up with what is generally known as the Ptolemaic System; and this, compared with antique views of the shape of the world, was a great scientific advance.

What is the shape of the world? What did the ancients think was the shape of the world? The best general discussion I know is that very learned work of Dr Robert Eisler, published in 1910, called *Weltenmantel und Himmelszelt*. Dr Eisler is surely right in warning us against the assumption, so commonly made, that the ancients, and notably the writers of the Old Testament, conceived of anything like the Ptolemaic system with its orderly arrangement of concentric revolving spheres. What they thought of was more like a tent with its supporting pillars or framework. Indeed the diagrams in the work of Cosmas Indicopleustes, a writer of the sixth century who rejected the Ptolemaic scheme as being un-Biblical, shew us the world as not unlike a 'Saratoga trunk'. Up above, covered by a curved top, was the Kingdom of Heaven. Below was the Earth, with pillars at the corners supporting the heavens. The Sun goes round and round from the East to the South, then to the West, and then to the North behind the great Mountain (the shadow of which causes Night), and so to the East again.

It is not necessary to consider this ancient view of the world in any detail. The important thing is to recognize, as Eisler does (p. 631), that the choice between the two theories, that which regarded the Earth as a ball and that which regarded it as the flat floor of a tent, was not between two rival myths but between what we nowadays call Science and Religion. The strength of what may be called the Tent-view lay in ancient tradition, in its easy allegorization, in the obvious analogy between this view of the Universe and a human dwelling; the strength of the Ball-view lay solely in its better agreement with observed facts.

Towards the end of the first century of our era this new, scientific, 'Ptolemaic' view of the world had come to be held by most cultivated persons in much the same sort of way as most cultivated persons now believe in 'Evolution'. There were difficulties, of course. If the Earth were a sphere and there were men at the antipodes, would they not fall off? This, and other similar questions, then unanswerable, were often put. But there remained always the impressive spectacle of the fixed stars, revolving night after night round the Pole. These, at least, once their invariable configuration had been noted, must be thought of as fixed in a rigid though transparent sphere rotating round the Earth. And if the stars are fixed in a sphere of this kind it seemed reasonable to explain the more unaccountable movements of the other heavenly bodies in a similar way. There must be similar spheres for the Sun and for the Moon and for the Five Planets, with this difference, however, that these were not fixed at a particular point on their sphere. Or else, if so fixed, their several spheres revolved irregularly.

The point which is of importance for us is this, that in any case men's thoughts had come to conceive of the Earth on which they lived as surrounded by crystal, transparent, but rigid, spheres, very much as the heart of an onion is encased by its outer layers. This view immensely enhanced the importance of each planet. It was no longer a tiny point of light mysteriously wandering among the other heavenly bodies. To the believer in the Ptolemaic astronomy it was the Lord of a Sphere which encased the Earth itself. If it was high or low above the ground, nearer or further from other heavenly bodies, it seemed reasonable to suppose that it exerted a special influence on the Earth and its inhabitants. And along with this belief there was another, intimately bound up with the scientific character of the Ptolemaic system. 'Planets' might indeed be 'wandering stars', and the rules of their courses were very imperfectly known even to the most learned astronomers, but the very observations that had led to the excogitation of the system had taught the comparative regularity and inevitableness with which the heavenly bodies, planets included, do move. If then the planets (or their spheres) had an influence on men, that influence came inevitably and inexorably. Astrology as a doctrine is a doctrine of Fate, of inevitable and inexorable Fate.

SOMA—SEMA

We shall come back to Astrology, but it will be convenient to go on now to another leading idea of cultivated thought in late Pagan times. It is most conveniently formulated in a Greek catchword, σῶμα σῆμα, 'the body a tomb'.[1]

What does this imply? I think, in the first place, that the *soma-sema* doctrine may be described as the reverse or back-view of 'the Immortality of the Soul'. The immortality of the human soul is not a doctrine taught in the Bible, either in the Old or the New Testament. GOD alone 'hath immortality'. He may confer it on others, but it is no

[1] A modern expression of the same idea is to be found in Schleiermacher's exclamation 'All who belong to a better world must for the present pine in dismal servitude' (*Schleiermacher's Soliloquies*, ed. H. L. Friess, p. 56).

necessary and natural postulate of human existence. A vivid belief in GOD's justice, a belief that
the GOD of all the earth will in the end do right, led
most Jews to believe, from the time of the Macca-
baean rising onwards, that martyred saints would
not be unrewarded and that notorious sinners and
persecutors, such as Antiochus Epiphanes, would
receive in their own persons the due punishment
for their evil deeds. So arose the belief in the
Resurrection of the Dead. It is a moral doctrine,
not a physical theory. The Greek notion of the
immortality of the soul, on the other hand, is not
in itself moral but logical and psychological. 'It
must be so,' says Addison's Cato, 'Plato, thou
reasonest well'; these well-known words most faithfully describe the nature of the notion and its
intellectual basis.

The soul of man, then, the *Psyche*, the queer
inhabitant of the human body that in dreams seems
to be able to wander outside at will, only to be
imperiously called back on waking, was held by
many Greeks to be immortal. But it was tied to a
mortal body, like a bird in a cage. This body was of
earth, of the same or similar substance as stones
and mud and other inanimate things. The soul, on
the other hand, was 'ethereal'—what does that
mean? It meant that its true nature and abode was
the Upper Air, in the pure region high above the
clouds. The body enclosed it like a tomb: if only
the body were dissolved, the immortal soul was
free to mount up to its true home.

How did this group of ideas stand to Astrology and the victorious Ptolemaic system? The Ptolemaic system had brought in the Spheres, translucent walls of crystal cutting off Earth from Heaven beyond, cutting off the Soul in its upward flight. How could the Soul get through?

My point in emphasizing the Ptolemaic system and the *soma-sema* view of human life thus at the outset of our study of Gnosticism is that these two things are something wider and more general than any of the 'Mystery-Religions', something wider and more general than the reconstructed speculations of a Posidonius. As I said just now, a view of the Universe conditioned by these two ideas corresponds more or less to the position that an evolutionary philosophy has with us. It is quite possible to retain belief in an old religion without much reference to these things, but a new religion or a new philosophy will have had to take account of them.

MAGIC

One other factor in many Gnostic systems calls for notice here. This is Magic and the use of magical or 'barbarous' names. We shall hear of Barbelo, of Ialdabaoth, of Aberamenthōu, not to mention Sabaoth and Melchisedec and other genuine Biblical words. How are we to regard these?

It should be remembered that there is a whole branch of study, often called 'Gnostic', which has really very little directly to do with Valentinus and

Basilides and other such Christian thinkers, I mean
the study of so-called 'Gnostic' gems and charms.
Some of the names and figures on these gems, e.g.
Abrasax, play a part in some Gnostic systems, but
there is no evidence that the gems were once owned
by Valentinians or Basilidians. Some of the gems
may be even older than the Christian era, and in any
case I do not think that they have very much to do
with Gnosticism in our sense of the word. There
are also magical texts on papyrus, which are akin
to the gems, but hardly belong to any Christian
Gnostic school.

What the outlandish names in magical formulae
and on gems attest is the belief, from which the
Bible is almost free, that the use of particular
names or syllables will cause the Deity or the
Demon to attend to an invocation. And it seems
the general rule among all nations, including the
Greeks notwithstanding their general contempt
for 'barbarians', that foreign, outlandish names
were considered the most potent. Let us begin by
the familiar word *Sabaoth*. There can be little doubt
that this is merely the Hebrew for 'hosts' or
'armies', and that the ancient Israelites spoke of
their GOD as the God of the hosts of Israel (see
e.g. Amos iii 13, vi 14). But the phrase יהוה צבאות
was in some of the more ancient (and worse translated) parts of the Greek Bible rendered by ΚΥΡΙΟC
CΑΒΑѠΘ, notably in the Book of Isaiah. This seems
to have been understood by persons ignorant of
Hebrew to mean the Lord Sabaoth, a Divine Per-

sonage whose Name was Sabaoth.[1] Wherever,
therefore, we find the name, or personage, or
emanation, or deity, called Sabaoth, we may infer,
firstly, a knowledge of the Greek Bible (generally,
no doubt, at second or third hand); and secondly,
ignorance of Hebrew. Where we find the proper
name Sabaoth we must beware of ascribing any
Jewish origin to the beliefs or traditions (for Jews
would know better), and at the same time we
are in touch with circles that ascribed value and
potency to names found in the Old Testament in
Greek. In other words these circles were neither
Jewish nor Pagan, but some sort of Christian.

Let me illustrate this conclusion by a counter-
illustration. When GOD appeared to Moses, according to the story told in Exodus, and Moses
asked Him what His Name was, GOD said 'I will
be what I will be'. It is clearly a sort of play upon
one pronunciation of the Tetragrammaton, and its
meaning in the context may be safely deduced from
the 'Certainly *I will be* with thee' of Exod. iii 12.
The Septuagint has for the mysterious phrase ἐγώ
εἰμι ὁ ὤν, 'I am He that is'. This is sufficiently
impressive and philosophical, even if philologically
inaccurate. But it is useless for Magic. The magi-
cian, the man who occupied himself in transcribing
spells which would compel the unseen Powers to
listen, was not interested in the nature of Being
or in ontological speculation. He wanted a com-
pelling formula. On the other hand the Peshitta,

[1] See on this Epiphanius, *Haer.* XXVI, p. 92.

i.e. the Syriac translation of the Hebrew Bible, transcribed the Hebrew syllables, making *Ahyah-asharahyah*: this word is meaningless in Syriac, and therefore is much used in Syriac charms.[1]

Side by side with *Sabaoth*, which is a genuine Hebrew word unintelligently used, may be placed *Ialdabaoth*, which in some Gnostic systems is the name of the Demiurge. No proper derivation for this name can be found: I doubt if any rational derivation ever existed. It seems to me to be formed after the analogy of Sabaoth. Possibly also the first inventor of the name had heard that *Iald* or *Yeled* meant 'child' or 'boy' and that *Ab* or *Abba* meant 'father'. But the rules of philology, which are undeviating in genuine natural formations, do not hold for artificial names.[2]

Taking the magical names as a whole, it is pretty clear that we can divide them into three main classes. There are the names just considered, which are accurate or inaccurate Biblical words. Then there are genuine non-Biblical names, whether of Gods or men. Of these perhaps the most curious is the Babylonian Goddess of the Underworld *Eresh-ki-gal*, who appears in the Leiden Papyrus as ερεϲχιϯαλ, and on a gem as ερεχιϯαϯ.[3] It is worth while to lay some stress on this isolated fact, for *Erechigag* on the gem looked very much

[1] See e.g. H. Gollancz, *The Book of Protection*, §§ 4, 5.

[2] Personally, I find it difficult to separate Ialdabaoth altogether from ιαω ϲαβαωθ, but neither in sound nor in writing does -λα- resemble -ωϲ-.

[3] C. W. King, *The Gnostics and their Remains*, p. 318.

like one of the many nonsense-names which form
the third class. Another non-Biblical name is the
God *Chnoub* or *Chnoum* (another form of 'Anubis'),
figured like a worm or snake with a crest—probably a sort of cobra-form. It is noteworthy that
neither 'Ereshkigal' nor 'Khnum' plays any part in
Christian Gnostic angelology. On the other hand
ⲁⲃⲉⲣⲁⲙⲉⲛⲑⲱⲟⲩ, which occurs with Ereshkigal in
the Leiden Papyrus, is equated in *Pistis Sophia*
with Jesus. In the next chapter a provisional derivation of *Aberamenthōu* will be put forward.

But besides these two classes of names, which,
however much corrupted, do represent a real terminology, we meet on gems and in some Gnostic books
with mere nonsense-names, often unpronounce-
able, such as the name of the 'True God' in the
Books of Ieu, viz. Ioeiaōthōuikhōlmiō, or con-
sisting of all the vowels in succession. These names
sometimes read both ways, like Ablanathanalba,
or another of 59 letters which is said to be a name
of 'Khnūb'! Some of these nonsense-names may,
as I have just said, be corruptions of real words,
but we must allow for an element of mere jingle and
mystification. In parts of *Pistis Sophia* and other
Gnostic works in Coptic there are a good many of
these nonsense-names: it is beside the mark to seek
for derivations, unless they recur in different works
with some stability of form. My chief reason for
bringing these names forward at this point is to
insist that they are not peculiar to works or systems
which have some claim to be classed as Christian

Gnostic, but are a general feature of magical literature.

THE TWO KINDS OF GNOSTIC LORE

All this being premised, we come at last to the main Gnostic documents, and it is easy to see that they fall into two classes. There is a Gnosticism which is mainly a philosophy, and there is a Gnosticism which is mainly a mythology. In the first class the terms are mainly Greek, in the second class the terms are largely pseudo-Hebraic, akin to the names used in Magic.

Which of these classes is the more original and which derivative? The question is different from the more general one which asks Which comes first, Magic or Religion? A very slight acquaintance with our Gnostic writings is enough to shew that they all have the same general aim, and that is to present the rôle of Jesus in a new way. The presentations are most diverse, and some of them are to our taste childish, but in the opinion of their authors they were something satisfactory, more satisfactory than the common account. In other words, they are not developments of Religion in general, but explanations of the particular mystery presented by Christianity. Only a philosophy can explain a mystery: a mythology may embody a philosophy, but does not in itself explain it. For this reason I regard the more or less philosophical Gnosticism—that is to say, Valentinus—as original and the mythological Gnosticism as on the whole derivative and degenerate. The mythological *tale* of the Fall of Sophia is a mere embodiment of the philosophical *notion* as it appears in Valentinus's system.

One isolated point from the tracts associated with *Pistis Sophia* is worth notice by the way. No doubt these Coptic documents are later and derivative, but they have the advantage of being complete, and certain ideas are there preserved which are not equally preserved in the accounts we possess of earlier Gnostic systems, simply because they afforded no controversial point to orthodox apologists. I am especially thinking of the use of the Coptic word ϲⲕⲩⲗⲗⲓ ⲙⲙⲟⲓ in the *Pistis Sophia* literature. This word is an adaptation of σκύλλεσθαι, 'to trouble oneself'.[1] Because men were sinners they were in trouble, but Jesus in the highest Heaven 'troubled Himself' about them, and so came down to bring them the means of salvation. The Gnostic cannot explain why this came to pass, any more than the Catholic, but both Gnostic and Catholic recognize it as the foundation of their belief. They differ considerably about the nature of sin and defilement, they differ about the human body of Jesus and its nature, but they agree about the Divine Compassion and that its embodiment was found in Jesus the Saviour.

[1] As in μὴ σκύλλου, Lk. vii 6. This explanation of the Coptic word, first pointed out in *Journ. Theol. Stud.* xxiii, p. 272, has been adopted by Schmidt in his revised translation (1925): Schmidt now renders it 'sich abmühen'.

PHILOSOPHICAL GNOSTICISM

VALENTINUS

I begin with Valentinus, for the same reason as
S. Irenaeus does, because of his general importance.
Here at least we have a thinker, who impressed the
Christian world, though in the end the Catholic
Church rejected the special form in which he and
his disciples expressed his doctrine. His name was
known all over the Christian churches from the
Euphrates to the Rhône: he is the only Gnostic,
except Marcion, named by Aphraates.

At the beginning of the great work of Irenaeus[1]
an account is given of the Valentinian theory of
the origin of things. Valentinus taught that there
was an original *Forefather* (Προπάτωρ), called also
The Deep (Βυθόσ). With this primordial essence
dwelt a *Thought* ("Εννοια), called also *Grace* (Χάρισ),
for it was not conditioned, and *Silence* (Σιγή), for
it made no sign of its existence. Somehow the
immeasurable Deep made its own Thought fecund,
and so *Mind* (Νοῦσ) came into being; and though it
was called *Unique* (Μονογενήσ) it had a correlative
side to it called *Truth* ('Αλήθεια). It will be noticed
that the Pairs are very much like the Hegelian
Thesis and Antithesis that between them bring
forth a Synthesis. In other words, the Valentinian
heavenly hierarchy, known as the Pleroma, is not
in essence Mythology but Philosophy. After all,
human beings only know of two kinds of fresh

[1] Irenaeus, *adv. Haer.* I i, 1–3 (Harvey, pp. 8 ff.): see
Journ. Theol. Stud. xxv, pp. 64–7.

42

production: there is the thought or idea that seems to be self-produced from a man's consciousness, and there is the new individual that comes from generation in plants and animals. By the first process the ultimate Forefather of Valentinian theology conceived His original Thought, and by something analogous to the second the dumb Thought produced what could be called *Nous*. In other words Nous was 'begotten, not made'. 'Nous' is an intelligent Understanding, the inevitable counterpart of which is Truth. For if there be nothing true to understand there can be no intelligent understanding.

It must also be pointed out that the original *Bythos*, the hidden Deep that produced the first Thought out of itself, corresponds in many ways to the Subliminal Self as conceived by some modern psychologists. What I mean is well put in Dr Sanday's book, *Christologies Ancient and Modern.* Whether we use the phraseology of the older school which talks about 'unconscious cerebration',[1] or the newer one which uses the term 'Subliminal Self',[2] there is in the human personality an inner cornucopia, a treasure-house, something within us more 'profound', impulses good and bad which 'come flickering up from below',[3] in a word there is from time to time a 'thought' or 'notion' which proceeds not so much from our conscious reason-

[1] See Sanday, p. 192.
[2] Sanday, p. 140 (quoting F. W. H. Myers).
[3] Sanday, p. 157.

ing powers as from what is sometimes called 'the abysmal depths of personality'. Abysmal is a word often misused, but here it is technically correct; it corresponds to the Valentinian word *Bythos*. It was by a process analogous to that by which new notions come into our minds out of the unknown activities of our unconscious selves that the Valentinian 'Forefather' produced His first unexpressed Thought. I have elaborated this analogy at some length, because I wish to point out that the ideas of Valentinus are not so very far removed from some of the conceptions of modern thinking, different as is the terminology.

Many more pairs according to Valentinus were formed in this way, the last of which was *Design* (Θελητόσ) and *Wisdom* (Σοφία). For the last name I venture to suggest a change from the usual English rendering. As we are soon to learn, Sophia's conduct was not marked by true Wisdom: what in modern terminology would be a much nearer equivalent is *Philosophy*. The name of her consort may best be seen from Malachi iii 12, where the Holy Land in which GOD takes pleasure (*'éreṣ ḥēpheṣ*) is called γῆ θελητή. So here, GOD took pleasure in the consort of Sophia, he was her '*Intended*'.

But according to Valentinus what was intended did not take place. The first Forefather was not visible to the whole family of Aeons: He could properly be perceived by Nous alone, by the pure Intelligence. But somehow Sophia got a glimpse of this exalted Forefather, and she desired to have direct intercourse with Him. This was not intended for her: her search for the Unsearchable was labour and sorrow, and, to continue the tale, her unauthorized passion somehow made her fecund with a formless monster. In pain and terror Sophia cried out for help to be sent to her from the Father and all the Aeons, and the Father sent to her a new Being called *Horos*, who separated her from the monster that she had conceived, and restored her to her proper condition among the Aeons. Her monstrous offspring, on the other hand, fell outside the heavenly Society (the Pleroma) altogether, and became the cause of this sensible and material world.

I have dropped into Myth, as Valentinus does, but it is quite evident all the time that he is describing the first origin of things under the figure of a myth, and not only the origin of things but also the mixture of good and evil found in this our world; and further, that his idea of the origin of things was psychological, akin to the mental processes of our own mind, which indeed are the only mental processes we know of. 'Sophia', as I said, is Philosophy. Philosophy sometimes seems to have a glimpse of the Deep, that is, of Ultimate Reality: it desires to have direct touch with Ultimate Reality. The vision of what is ultimate is entrancing but intoxicating: Philosophy cannot conceive it intelligently and produces only disordered Fancies.[1] What physician, or rather surgeon, can treat the disordered fancies of Philosophy? Valentinus's name for him is *Horos*, i.e. 'Boundary', in other words true Definition.

Here we come to the most interesting, and at the same time the most Christian, feature of Valentinian doctrine. Horos, we are told, had other names meaning Emancipator, Redeemer, etc., but it is also called 'Cross' (σταυρόσ), because it 'crucified away' (ἀποσταυρωθῆναι) the disordered fancy of Philosophy. This is nothing more nor less than the Pauline doctrine that the believer in Christ Jesus has 'crucified' the flesh with the affections (παθήματα) and lusts,[2]—a point that has often been missed by expounders of the Valentinian system, who have been driven to suppose that by σταυρόσ, the common word for Cross, familiar to every Christian, Valentinus meant 'stake' or 'paling', and that what Horos did was to fence Sophia off from her offspring! But the discovery of the *Acts of John* makes the interpretation given above certain. In that work, which is itself a product of 'Gnostic' ways of thought, we are told that the real effective Cross is the marking-off (διορισμόσ) of all things.[3] Further, it seems that the figure thought of is not + but T—something which divides everything below it into 'right' and

[1] The word used by Valentinus is *Enthymesis*.

[2] Gal. v 24.

[3] See M. R. James, *Apocryphal N.T.* §§ 98–100 = 'Acts of John' xiii in *Apocrypha Anecdota*, II.

'left', but above it there is no division. We know
from other sources, e.g. from the 'Epistle of
Barnabas', chap. ix, that when Early Christians
thought of the shape of the Cross it was as something like the letter **T** rather than the shape we now
conventionally give to it.

The essence of Christianity is contained in the
Cross and what Christians have associated with the
Cross. No religious theory that does not contain
a doctrine of the Cross has a right to the name
'Christian'. But from the beginning it was a stumbling-block, a 'scandal'. Here we see how Valentinus incorporates the Cross as the decisive factor
in his drama of salvation: it is just this that makes
his heresy, however erratic and however heretical,
a *Christian* heresy.

It will not be necessary to follow in any detail
the further ramifications of Valentinian cosmogony; of the production of the heavenly pre-
existent Jesus by all the Aeons, so that He has the
virtues of all of them; of the stages in the production of the visible world and of the world of
men; of the ultimate redemption of 'Achamoth'
(for so they named the Disordered Fancy of
Sophia) and of those of her offspring who attained
to some measure of true knowledge (γνῶσιο)[1]. It
will not be necessary, for in the evolution, the fall,
and the subsequent reinstatement of 'Sophia' or
Philosophy, the essential ideas of Valentinus are
expressed.

[1] *Iren.* (ed. Harvey, p. 53 = M 29).

The two points I wish to emphasize are that these ideas are essentially philosophical, not mythological; and that they are an attempt at formulating a *Christian* philosophy. Not indeed that it was a philosophy in the Socratic sense, of which I spoke in the previous discourse. It is from that point of view thoroughly 'gnostic' and authoritarian. But I feel that it is a thoughtful attempt to express the ever-recurring problems of philosophy in accordance with something very like the Christian view of things by means of concepts borrowed from the processes of human thought. *Unde malum, et quare? Unde homo, et quomodo?* And, *Unde Deus?*[1] The last question, Tertullian adds, especially concerns the Valentinians.

In this Tertullian is not quite fair. Valentinus does not ask whence the primordial Forefather came, the Cause and Origin of everything. What he was concerned with was the problem of how Two could come from the original undifferentiated One, how the multifarious world, multifarious and variegated both in thought and sense, could have originated from the One original Existence. He solves it by telling his disciples that a sort of Thought or Notion of it came up out of the depth of the Forefather's being, just as notions swim into our own consciousness. The Forefather considered His Notion, He had now Something to contemplate: He understood it, and what He understood was the truth. There was now both

[1] Tert. *de Praescriptione*, VII.

48

Understanding and something to understand, *Nous* and *Aletheia*. The natural result, κατὰ φύσιν, of this family of ideas was a whole brood of fairly distinct conceptions, harmoniously developing from the original notion.

So far, so good. But now we come to the story of Sophia, to the collapse of Philosophy. In Biblical language we have advanced as far as Gen. i 31, or the fourth verse of the Fourth Gospel. We must remember that Valentinus was a Christian, that to him Jesus was the Saviour, and that 'Saviour' implies something to be 'saved'. What was Valentinus's doctrine of the Fall?

There is no intellectual necessity for the fall of Sophia, but Valentinus, both as a Greek and as a Christian, believed in the empirical fact. As a Greek he held the *soma-sema* theory, viz. that the better, 'ethereal', part of him was imprisoned in gross matter; while as a Christian he found a doctrine of the Fall of Man, from the effects of which the Son of God had come down to earth to deliver those who received Him. Like Mani after him, he felt that the Fall must have happened in essence before this world, this mixed world, came into being. The world is the *result* of the Fall, not a regrettable accident which occurred soon after it came into being.

Let us remember that orthodox Christian speculation has also, in its own fashion, attempted to go behind the story of the Fall of Adam. 'The Serpent beguiled me': obviously, therefore, Christians

49

came to think of the Serpent of Genesis as a demon, as Satan, as Lucifer. How then are we to explain the fall of Lucifer? What was the first sin? The oldest answer given to this question, a pre-Christian answer supplied by the Book of Enoch, makes the sin of fallen Angels to be *Lust*, because they saw the daughters of Man that they were fair. But this is no answer at all, for Adam and Eve had already been expelled from Paradise before the daughters of Men were born. The great opponent of Valentinus had a different theory: the sin of Lucifer was *Envy* of Man created in the image of God.[1] Man, according to this preposterous idea, was the innocent cause of his own misfortunes. Psychologically less unsatisfactory is the theory, championed especially by S. Augustine, that the sin of Lucifer was *Pride*, and that his pride came (like the original Thought of the Forefather) from his own being. This is a better theory, because it is not concerned with this human world at all: 'evil', though latent, was already in existence when man came into being.

The theory of Valentinus is somewhat similar to this, but it combines a certain element of the first theory. What was the sin of Sophia, for which she herself and her irregular offspring paid so dear? What is 'Lust'? Essentially it is unregulated desire. What is 'Pride'? A self-confidence not borne out by facts. Sophia had had a glimpse of

[1] Irenaeus, *adv. Haer.* IV (Harvey, II, p. 303): see also a Note by W. Crum in *J.T.S.* IV, p. 396.

something better than she had been able to imagine,
and she wanted it for herself: Philosophy has an
inkling of the ultimate Reality, but cannot and does
not properly conceive it, and so gives birth to what
I have called 'disordered fancies', which had better
not have been ever conceived. Yet once these
fancies have come into being the ultimate Intelligence which orders everything is able and willing
to bring good out of evil. Philosophy can be
refined and purified, and all that is good in the
disordered fancies will ultimately find a place in
the universal harmony. And further, according to
Valentinus, this is somehow accomplished by the
Cross.

I feel certain that the system of Valentinus, as
formulated by Ptolemaeus and summarized by
Irenaeus,[1] was consciously a *Christian* philosophy,
designed to exhibit the essential truth of the
Christian Religion to Greek-thinking men who
regarded the *soma-sema* theory of human life as
obvious, and who desired to have their religion
freed from the materialistic shackles of a barbarian
allegory.

I use the word 'allegory', because Valentinus, at
least as represented by Ptolemaeus his disciple,
seems not so much to try to supersede the Scriptures of the Old and New Testaments as to interpret them. Of course he is profoundly unhistorical
and entirely arbitrary according to our ideas of true
interpretation, but he seems to have thought that

[1] Irenaeus, *adv. Haer.* I, pp. 5, 80.

he was really giving the true meaning, as when, for instance, he declares that by Christ and the Woman with an Issue is signified the passion of Sophia and her cure, for the 'virtue' which went forth from Jesus was that Horos-Stauros, which separated her from her pathological issue.[1] Valentinus has all the more right to allegorize in this way, inasmuch as the theory of the heavenly Aeons, their production and the fall of one of them with its subsequent redemption, is an universal process, a mirror of all concrete happenings, somewhat after the manner of the universality, according to Hegel, of thesis and antithesis.

It seems to me that there is very little Mythology in the Valentinian theology. 'Sophia' is not a sort of Angel, but means philosophy or rather philosophic theology. Even in the orthodox diction of the Creeds we talk about 'begotten', but mean something less materialistic than the term naturally implies. Valentinus is no more materialistic in intention than the Nicene Creed, and in judging him to-day we ought to be as sympathetic to his phraseology as we are to the wording of the historic Creeds.

The chief difference between Valentinus and the orthodox was that the orthodox theology was much more careful to retain Biblical terms. The Church, with a true instinct, was afraid of mythology: in the sequel we shall see that it had good reason to be

[1] Irenaeus (Harvey, I, p. 27).

afraid. Churchmen had reason to be afraid not so
much of Valentinus, as of what Valentinianism
would inevitably lead to.

THE BARBELO-GNOSTICS

The account of Valentinus's doctrine given above
follows the description given by S. Irenaeus, who
appears to follow the account given by one
Ptolemaeus, a disciple of Valentinus, no doubt the
same as the Ptolemaeus who wrote the 'Epistle to
Flora'. Another branch of the same, or very
similar, teaching should be mentioned here. This
is the sect or sects whose doctrines are described by
Irenaeus at the end of his first Book (1 29).[1] The
text of Irenaeus is here preserved in the Latin
translation, which we know to be an extremely
faithful and literal rendering, and it is also re-
produced by Theodoret in Greek, not always with
perfect accuracy. But in addition to Irenaeus we
now have fragments of the original from which
Irenaeus drew his information. They are to be
found in a Coptic MS which has been at Berlin for
the last 35 years and is not even now published, but
a very full account of it was given by Carl Schmidt
in 1907 in the volume called *Philotesia*.[2] The Coptic
fragments are often obscure, but they contain the
exposition of a theology, not its confutation.

The true title of this work, not given by

[1] Harvey, I, pp. 221–6.
[2] *Philotesia*, a Festschrift in honour of Paul Kleinert
(Berlin, 1907), pp. 317–36.

Irenaeus, is the '*Apocryphon* of John', i.e. the secret revelation given to S. John the Apostle, a similar title to that of the canonical Apocalypse. Jesus appears in a vision to John and reveals Himself as 'the Father, the Mother, and the Son', in a word as the unmixed Godhead, the cause of all things. It will not be necessary to describe the system fully: three points only need to be considered, viz. the name of the All-Mother, the origin of Evil, and the central rôle of 'Jesus'.

The name of the All-Mother is *Barbelo*. The original Source of all things, corresponding to the Valentinian *Bythos* or Deep, is depicted as dwelling in His own clear and tranquil Light, which is the Fountain of the Water of Life. Out of the depths of His own pure essence comes His own Ἔννοια or Thought, just as in the system of Valentinus, but She is given (without explanation) the name *Barbelo*. It is not the only 'barbaric' name in the 'Apocryphon of John', but it is in many ways the most noteworthy. Unlike *Sabaoth* (and its corruptions) it does not appear to come directly or indirectly from the Old Testament, indeed it does not appear to have a Semitic derivation. It is also worth remark that Barbelo is always a kindly, sympathetic personage. Ialdabaoth and Sabaoth, Demiurge and Archon, often come before us as the names of heavenly Tyrants, rebels like Lucifer against the Supreme GOD and tyrants to man, but Barbelo is never so degraded. I have ventured elsewhere to conjecture that the word 'Barbelo' is adapted from the Coptic *belbile*, a 'seed' or 'grain', so that while Greek speculation traced the first beginnings of things to a Thought or Notion the more concrete Egyptian mind thought of a Seed. In any case, with the name Barbelo we come to Egyptian, as distinct from merely Alexandrian ground, and we begin to pass from philosophy to mythology.[1]

The origin of Evil, or of Matter—the two to the Gnostic are almost synonymous—is similar to the Valentinian account. The trouble came through the misdirected desires of 'Sophia', but here Sophia is distinctly a more mythological figure than in the true Valentinian representation. She, like the other products of Barbelo, is spoken of by the revealing Jesus to John as 'our fellow-sister', but she failed to find her proper consort and the virtue that went out from her turned into a monster called Ialdabaoth, the First Archon, from whom in turn came the visible material Universe with all the ills that Gnostics associated with the visible material Universe. All this, of course, is in essential accordance with Valentinus, but we may notice the emergence of a new key-word, which is not, I think, found in Ptolemaeus. The trouble in Sophia came from τὸ προύνικον, the lustful disposition in her, according to the Coptic account,[2] while Irenaeus seems to understand that these Gnostics called Sophia herself ἡ Προύνικοσ. This term *Prunicus* is in any case

[1] See the separate Note, p. 58.
[2] *Philotesia*, p. 329.

a last relic of the psychological terminology of the earlier Christian Gnostics; in what follows it is all mythology.

Finally, the central rôle assigned to 'Jesus' in the *Apocryphon Iohannis* must be recognized. It is difficult not to go into some detail in explaining Gnostic theologies and cosmologies. The study is obscure, and yet fascinating to the investigator, but to the ordinary sensible man and woman of the twentieth century the detailed investigation of the alleged relation of imaginary beings to one another is apt to seem confusing if not tedious. We may therefore bring ourselves up at this point and ask what all this is about? What is the point of Barbelo-Gnosticism? What is the aim of the Gnostic writer who wrote the *Apocryphon Iohannis*?

Of course it may be answered that the aim is the propagation (among a suitable audience) of 'Gnosis', that it gives an answer to the great questions 'Whence comes evil and why?' 'Whence comes man and how?', once again to use Tertullian's famous words. But it is Jesus who is the revealer and the saviour. He is to John the full incorporation of the Godhead, and it is through His action that the Divine Spark in man is enabled in the end to escape from the evil in which it is enmeshed.

In other words this system, like every other system historically included under the name of Gnostic, considers itself to be Christian, to be a philosophy of Christianity, an exposition of Christianity in terms more enlightened, and therefore more true, than Christianity as understood by vulgar believers. The figure of 'Jesus who appeared in Judaea', to quote the phrase afterwards used by Mani, is central to it; without this figure the whole system falls to pieces.

'The Gnosis', to use the fashionable modern term, does not precede Christianity but is a new formulation of Christianity, as understood by some second-century Christians who shared the physical and biological ideas most widely spread among 'the educated classes' of the Mediterranean civilization of their day. What they had dropped from ordinary Christianity was Christian Eschatology, the belief that this world was quickly coming to an end by the advent of Jesus Christ to judge the living and the resurrected dead on this earth. This belief, explicable as an expression or development of the Jewish religion, was wholly alien to Greek thought. On the other hand the Gnostics had not, in their own opinion, rejected the Old Testament or the Gospel record, but they claimed to interpret it in their own sense. They considered that they had received an enlightenment which shewed them the true meaning that lay behind the sacred Writings which ordinary Christians misunderstood. Even Marcion derived an important element in his teaching from the story of Adam and Eve, though he regarded the God of Judaism as the enemy of Jesus. Without Christianity, without the growth and success of the Christian Church, there would have been no Gnosticism. The various forms of Gnosticism are attempts to reformulate and express the ordinary Christianity in terms and categories which suited the science and philosophy of the day. And further, when we get behind the unfamiliar imagery to the ideas which they attempt to express, some of these forms are really thoughtful and shew kinship with some modern philosophical and psychological conceptions.

NOTE
ON THE NAME *BARBELO*

The name *Barbelo* (ⲃⲁⲣⲃⲏⲗⲱ) is given as the proper name of the First Thought or Notion (ἔννοια) of the Ultimate Forefather in the 'Apocryphon of John', which is also the work upon which the account in Irenaeus, *adv. Haer.* I 29 is based. It is also the name given for the corresponding personage by Epiphanius when describing the Simonians (*Haer.* XXI 56 *fin.*), the Nicolaitans (*Haer.* XXV 77 *med.*), and those called 'Gnostics' (*Haer.* XXVI 92 *init.*). Of these we may at once omit the Simonians, i.e. according to Epiphanius the followers of Simon Magus, because Epiphanius does not assert that they used the name Barbelo, but only that the Power which they call *Prunicus* is called by other heresies Barbero or Barbelo

(Βαρβηρὼ ἤτοι Βαρβηλώ): he obviously means the 'Gnostics' of *Haer.* xxvi.

Nicolaitans are in Epiphanius's terminology the followers of Nicolas of Antioch, the companion of Stephen, who was supposed to have fallen from grace and abandoned himself to an evil life. From what Epiphanius says in the second paragraph of *Haer.* xxv it is clear that there were no Nicolaitans directly derived from Nicolas, but Epiphanius groups a number of sects or schools as 'Nicolaitans' because they all practise a relaxed morality. Of these sects 'some', he says, use the name Barbelo. But it is all, so to speak, prefatory matter to what he has to say in *Haer.* xxvi about the 'so-called Gnostics', who were a sect with whom Epiphanius himself had dealings in his youth. I do not think it proved, therefore, that the name Barbelo is attested by Epiphanius except for these 'Gnostics'.

These Gnostics of *Haer.* xxvi were clearly domiciled in Egypt, apparently not far from Alexandria (τῆς πόλεωσ, p. 100 *med.*). The '*Apocryphon* of John' is preserved in a Coptic version, and it has various affinities with the *Pistis Sophia* literature and the Books of Jeū. It is reasonable therefore to postulate for it a geographically Egyptian origin, though it was doubtless composed in Greek. When therefore we find in these a term like *Barbelo*, which is neither Greek nor Semitic, it may be conjectured that its origin is Egyptian.

It is right to say at the outset that there can be no doubt about the spelling of the name as adopted by Gnostic theology. It is ⲃⲁⲣⲃⲏⲗⲱ in the *Apocryphon* of John, in *Pistis Sophia* and in the Latin version of Irenaeus. Theodoret has Βαρβηλώθ, but such appended letters to 'barbarous' names mean nothing, as in Sira*ch* and Aceldema*ch*. *Barbelo*, as it stands, means nothing, but we learn from Epiphanius that the name, as pronounced by his Egyptian Gnostic acquaintances, sounded as much like *Barbēro* as *Barbēlo* (Βαρβηρὼ ἤτοι Βαρβηλώ, p. 92 *init.*). This suggests that the true transcription of the liquids was uncertain, which is often the case in old Egyptian words, and is exemplified in one of the main differences between Fayyumic and other Egyptian dialects.

I suggest therefore that *Barbelo* is derived from the Coptic word ⲃⲗ̄ⲃⲓⲗⲉ, 'a seed', 'a single grain'. This word, like 'Barbelo', is feminine. It accords well with the concrete tendencies of Egyptian thought, in which (as in *Pist. Soph.* 121) a πνεῦμα could be bound to a bed, that the first product of the undifferentiated Deep, from which in due course all other things would come, should be regarded as a Seed, whereas to the more Hellenic imagination of Valentinus it was regarded as a Thought.

It is worth recording that, as noted above (p. 54), Barbelo is never represented as unfriendly to man. 'To Barbelo', says C. Schmidt (*Jeû*, p. 393), 'a hostile attitude to mankind is never

ascribed.' When therefore we read in *Pist. Soph.*
359 a prayer of Jesus for His Disciples that 'all the
powers of the Unseen God Agrammachamareg
and the Barbelo the Bdella' may be the reverse of
sinister we know something is wrong. ⲃⲁⲉⲗⲗⲁ
cannot be the Greek word βδέλλα, 'leech'. I venture to suggest (1) that in the letters ⲧⲃⲁⲣⲃⲏⲗⲱ
ⲧⲉⲃⲁⲉⲗⲗⲁ the first half is a correction of the
second, correct so far as the meaning goes, and (2)
that ⲧⲉⲃⲁⲉⲗⲗⲁ is a corrupt survival of another,
and really more correct, form of the name, viz.
ⲧⲉⲃⲗⲃⲓⲗⲁ or some such spelling.

I presume that the name of the 'Unseen God' is
a corruption of ἀγράμματοσ (in the sense of 'Not
to be expressed in letters'), modified by an effort to
make it repeat like 'Ablanathanalba', possibly with
a reminiscence of the ineffable 'Tetragrammaton' of
the Jews. It occurs elsewhere as *Akrammakram-
makanarissse.*

Chapter III

EGYPTIAN GNOSTIC WORKS

THE documents which we are to consider in this chapter are rather difficult to place. Ancient Egypt and the Egypt of the Graeco-Roman world perished finally with the Mohammedan Conquests. The curious amalgam presented by the Levantine civilization of Greek-speaking Alexandria has dissolved, and all that survives directly of the old Egypt is the Coptic Church. In earlier times, certainly down to the fifth century A.D., there was a more variegated intellectual life in Christian Egypt, and chance has preserved a few old documents of a very different character from the later literature of the Copts. The two chief documents came to England at the end of the eighteenth century: they are the Askew MS [1] containing *Pistis Sophia* with other writings, and the Papyri brought back by James Bruce. Both are ancient: the Askew MS is probably of the fifth century, for at a later date its transcription in Egypt is inconceivable and Prof. Carl Schmidt even suggests a date before 400. The Bruce Papyri, now at Oxford, were brought to Europe by the celebrated traveller James Bruce. They

[1] Called after a former possessor, Anthony Askew, M.D., who died in 1774.

consist of a number of papyrus leaves with Coptic
writing of about the same age as the Askew MS, if
not older. Schmidt, who has edited the texts,[1]
found that the leaves formed part of two different
works, viz. the first and second Books of *Jeu*
(ιεον), and an unnamed Gnostic work which it is
convenient to call *Setheus* (cноεѵс). The text of the
Askew MS was edited by Schwartze and Peter-
mann in 1851, but the best translation is again by
C. Schmidt in the book called *Pistis Sophia*, published in 1925. Schmidt distinguishes two works
in the Askew MS, viz. the three books called *Pistis
Sophia* (or 'The Rolls of the Saviour'), and an
anonymous Gnostic work which follows it. In
Schmidt's opinion the chronological order of
these works is (1) Setheus, (2) Jeu, (3) the Anonymous work, (4) *Pistis Sophia*. Of these 'Setheus'
is akin to the *Apocryphon of John* (see above,
pp. 53 ff.), but it is later and derivative, quoting
Scripture, even Ecclesiastes and Hebrews, and
does not need further notice here. I begin with
Pistis Sophia, as it may be used as an introduction
to the curious world of thought to which all
these works belong.

Let us begin by not expecting too much con-
sistency. We are dealing, in the last resort, with
the products of human fancy, a fanciful world,
'moulded to the heart's desire', in which the
religious imagination was not tied down to histori-

[1] C. Schmidt, *Gnostische Schriften...aus dem Codex Bru-
cianus* (T. und U. VIII 1, 2), Leipzig, 1892.

cal facts preserved in an authoritative Book. In these days I venture to think we are often not sufficiently grateful to the orthodox Catholic theologians who clung so doggedly to the literal truth of the Scriptures. We have found out that some things in the Bible are not, after all, historically true, and we are easily persuaded to contrast our scientific knowledge of the Solar System, of the geological age of our Earth, of the wonderful vistas of ancient Oriental History, with the cramped ideas of the Church Fathers, drawn from the Bible. But we ought never to forget that the alternative to the Bible in the days we are considering was not Prof. Breasted's Ancient History, or Huxley and Lyell's Geology, or the Astronomy of Newton and Copernicus. The alternative to the Bible was a mere fancy picture of the world we live in, whereas the Bible did after all give materials for constructing the course of events which led to the Jewish Religion and the religious ideas that were the intellectual atmosphere of the world in which Christ and the Apostles moved.

And further, there is a generous prejudice often felt in favour of those whom we know only by refutations. We can see that Hippolytus and Epiphanius, even Irenaeus, are prejudiced and not always intelligent. We have a kind of sentiment that there must have been more in the systems of their Gnostic opponents than the refutations of them give us to understand. If only we could hear the Gnostics speak for themselves! Was the whole controversy a case of a victory of prejudice over philosophy, of superstition over free thought? If 'the Gnostics' had triumphed, might not the result have been a more rational, a more intelligent, Christian orthodoxy? Well, such pessimistic doubts might easily be held in former centuries, even a hundred years ago. In the documents we are considering to-day we hear Gnosticism speaking for itself. It is a curious study, a study in what may be called 'free' thought, I mean thought very little controlled by external considerations or rational design. There are not wanting acute remarks, ingenious combinations, a few striking, even brilliant, ideas, but the whole is fantastic. It is like nothing so much as the unhappy abortion of Sophia in the Valentinian myth, the *Enthymesis* or 'disordered fancy' that was not in accordance with Design.

And there is one other feature which these Coptic documents present. In Valentinus's ideas, especially as presented by his disciple Ptolemaeus and summarized by Irenaeus, we did seem in the presence of a thinker, who drew his notions (as the primordial Deep did of which he speaks) out of his inner consciousness. But in these Coptic documents there is a strong element of blind tradition, of accepting an idea and then mythologizing it. It is quite clear that if Valentinus had become a Doctor of the Church, it would not have saved the next generations from a superstitious and complicated mythology.

PISTIS SOPHIA

I will now give a short account of the Three Books of *Pistis Sophia*, confining myself mainly to the general structure of the work.[1] The scene is the Mount of Olives (4, 15, 169 ff., 171); the time, the eleventh year after the Resurrection. The idea is that Jesus the Saviour remained teaching the chief Disciples for twelve years after the Resurrection, after which they went forth to preach to the world: our book professes to record the last Revelation that Jesus gave them before His final retirement to the realms of light. This twelve-year sojourn of the Apostles near Jerusalem is no peculiarity of our book but a feature of general Christian tradition.[2]

On the 15th of Tybi, then, the moon being full, Jesus was clothed with a marvellous Robe of Light and straightway ascended into the highest Heaven: then He returned to the Disciples to give them a revelation of what He had done. First, He had modified the Fate on which Astrologers depend (26 ff.): He took away a third from the powers of the Rulers and made the spheres turn six months this way and six months that, so that in future

[1] The numbers refer to the Coptic pages of Schwartze-Petermann, which are repeated in the margins of all the editions.

[2] The ultimate source may be historical: it was about twelve years after the Crucifixion, in the reign of Herod Agrippa, that Peter was imprisoned in Jerusalem, escaped, and left the city (Acts xii).

astrologers cannot be sure of their horoscopes! Here Mary Magdalene interposes, recognizing that this is a fulfilment of Isaiah xix 3. Further, Jesus tells them (42) that as He ascended through the aeons—there are twelve comparatively material ones and a thirteenth above—He found the Pistis Sophia exiled from her proper place in the thirteenth aeon and subjected to the persecutions of the self-willed (αὐθάδησ) and disobedient Demon. This Sophia is the Valentinian Philosophy which had gone astray in its endeavour to get into direct touch with the supreme Reality,[1] but in our book the figure has become entirely personified and mythologized. Its fall has no inner rationality: it is merely a bit of esoteric doctrine to be accepted. Whatever the date of this writing may be, it is on quite another plane of thought to the system of Valentinus as expounded by Ptolemaeus. The myth itself remains; and a large section of our book, from which indeed it gets the name by which it is known in modern times, is occupied with it (43–181). In this section, no doubt, we have our author's own imagination at work and we see plainly how little there is of it. The only thing Pistis Sophia can do is to sing excessively dreary hymns, e.g. 'On thee, O light, have I hoped. Leave me not in the chaos, deliver me and save me according to thy knowledge. Give heed unto me and save me. Be unto me a saviour, O Light, and save me and lead me to thy light.... And in thy

---

[1] P. 45.

hands will I lay the purification of my light; thou hast saved me, O Light, according to thy knowledge' (84). Then Matthew comes forward and with remarkable perspicacity says to Jesus: 'My Lord, thy power hath prophesied thereof aforetime through David in the 30th Psalm, saying, On thee, O Lord, have I hoped. Let me never be put to shame, save me according to thy righteousness. Incline thine ear unto me and save me quickly. Be thou unto me a protecting God and a house of refuge to save me....Into thy hands I will render my spirit, thou hast redeemed me, O Lord, God of truth' (86). Of course one sees that the hymn of Pistis Sophia is simply made up out of the Psalm, the diction of which is much more concrete and varied. There are about twenty of these outpourings of Sophia, all constructed on the same lines, and all equally jejune in expression.

As I say, in this section we see the Coptic author of the book at work. The text of the quoted Psalms is that of the Ṣaʿidic Psalter.[1] The writer takes the text, alters it by turning most words like 'Lord' or 'God' into 'Light' (or occasionally into 'Saviour'), and words like 'shame' or 'misfortune' into 'Chaos'. This would be tolerable if done once or twice, but it is done at length a score of times. The principle, indeed, is good Gnostic exegesis, for even in the earliest Valentinian doctrine sayings and incidents in the Old and New

[1] There are occasional variations, especially in *Pistis Sophia* 86–110, but nothing of importance calls for remark.

Testaments are interpreted to be adumbrations of events in the Valentinian cosmogony. What is peculiar to these paraphrases in *Pistis Sophia* is the dull way in which they are composed. Valentinus invented the passion and the deliverance of Sophia, and then ingeniously saw an adumbration or cryptic allusion to it in the story of our Lord and the Woman with an issue:[1] the author of *Pistis Sophia* merely takes a Biblical Psalm and paraphrases it to be a hymn for 'Sophia' to sing.

It may be remarked that the name *Pistis-Sophia* is itself a 'barbarous' formation, not properly paralleled in Greek. There is some evidence that the Gnostic 'Sophia' (philosophy) was also named by other Gnostics 'Pistis' (faith): it is only in Coptic that we find the names run together. Similarly we have 'Zorokothora-Meljisedek' (*Pistis Sophia* 369, *sic*) run together; Melchisedec, whose genealogy is not given in the Bible, is identified, not with Shem as the Jews sometimes do, but with the heathen Zoroaster, and the names are fantastically coupled. We may add that the functions assigned to Zorokothora-Meljisedek have nothing to do with those of the Biblical Melchisedec or the Persian Zoroaster! Only the mere names were borrowed by the Gnostic.

But a demonstration that the immediate author or authors of the 'gnostic' documents included in the Askew MS was a rather stupid Copt does not exhaust the interest of the documents themselves.

[1] See above (chap. II, p. 52).

Our Copt cannot have lived later than the fifth century: he must have been more or less contemporary with Epiphanius, who died in 403. We have in the hymns of Sophia the measure of our Copt's intellectual feebleness, and there is much in the rest of the same quality. When therefore we find picturesque narrative or notable thoughts we may fairly put it down to some other earlier and more acute mind, whether that of Valentinus or of another. The interest of the book known as *Pistis Sophia* consists in this, that here and there such interesting and more ancient matter is preserved in it.

One isolated point of interest is to be found in the work of the compiler of Sophia's hymns. Most of them are founded on the Psalms of David, but in five instances they are founded on the Odes of Solomon. These Odes are extant in a Syriac translation, but appear to have been composed in Greek in free imitation of the Greek Psalter. It is likely that our Copt may have found them added as an appendix to the Canonical Psalter. The date of these Odes is much disputed, but the use of the ' 19th Ode' by Lactantius shews that the collection was known and esteemed in Nicomedia at the end of the third century. That they should have been known and esteemed in Egypt two or three generations later is therefore not abnormal. The existence of the Nitrian MS of the Odes in Syriac (B.M. Add. 14538) indicates that the Syriac translation may have been made in Egypt itself: possibly they were originally composed in Egypt, but they shew no more affinity to the doctrines found in *Pistis Sophia* than the Psalms of David do.

Of picturesque narrative there is not much in *Pistis Sophia*, but one queer tale stands out by itself and is worth quoting. In *Pistis Sophia* 118 Jesus tells the Disciples that a great Light-power came from on high to help the Pistis Sophia, and another Light-power came out of Jesus Himself, and these two Powers met one another and became a great stream of Light. Mary, i.e. Mary Magdalene, then quotes Psalm lxxxiv,[1] and declares this meeting of the Light-powers to have been signified in the words 'Mercy and truth are met together, righteousness and peace have kissed each other'. On this, Mary the Mother of Jesus comes forward and asks to be allowed to give a further explanation. She says the Psalm-verse refers to Jesus Himself, and goes on to say (120): 'When thou wert little, before the Spirit came over thee, there came the Spirit from on high whilst thou wert with Joseph in a vineyard. It came to me in my house in thy likeness, and I had not recognized it and I thought it was thou. And the Spirit said to me "Where is Jesus my Brother, that I may meet him?" And when it said that, I was in doubt and thought it was a phantom come to tempt me. So I took it and bound it at the foot of the bed in my house, till I went out into the field to you, to thee and Joseph, and found you in the vineyard with

[1] Psalm lxxxv, according to the English reckoning.

71

Joseph putting up the stakes. And it came to pass that when thou heardest me tell the matter to Joseph thou didst understand and didst rejoice and say "Where is he, that I may see him, for I am waiting for him in this place". But when Joseph had heard thee say these words he was troubled, and we went back at once, we entered into the house and found the Spirit bound on the bed. And we looked at thee and it, and found thee like it; and the one that was bound on the bed was untied, he embraced thee and kissed thee and thou didst kiss him: you became one'.

A strange tale, no doubt taken from some previously existing uncanonical source. But it is noteworthy as illustrating a view of the Incarnation intermediate between that which regarded the union of GOD and Man as taking place at the Baptism in Jordan, and that which regarded it as complete at birth. It seems to me also to throw some light on the curious saying from the Gospel of Thomas, quoted in Hippolytus (*Haer.* v 7, p. 101), which says 'He who seeks me will find me in children from seven years old, for there I shall be manifested, hidden in the fourteenth aeon' (αἰῶνι). Hippolytus understands by 'the fourteenth aeon' the fourteenth year of a boy's age,[1] but when we find that the Light-power came to Jesus from above the Thirteenth Aeon, and that then this story of the earthly boyhood of Jesus is quoted, it does seem

[1] See e.g. Hieron. *in Eccl.* IV (quoted by C. Taylor, *Pirke Aboth*, 2nd ed. p. 150).

as if our prosaic Copt had been using previous non-'gnostic' material to eke out details in his tale of Sophia. It is a pity that very little is known of this 'Gospel of Thomas' or of its contents and scope.

The rest of the 'Rolls of the Saviour', and also the anonymous treatise at the end, is occupied by the fate of human souls after death. Here we may go back to what I said at the beginning of Chapter II about the ideas or prejudices which permeated the Graeco-Roman world generally, and especially the two great ideas or notions of the Ptolemaic system and of the body as a prison or tomb for the human soul. The general scheme set forth in *Pistis Sophia* is much the same as must be the case in any theology dominated by these ideas. At death the soul is separated from the body and flies upward, but it has to pass through the crystal spheres which surround the earth; unless it is provided with the requisite passports the various guardians of the spheres will not let it through, and it is liable to be cast back and imprisoned again in a material body.

It should be noted that, as in the New Testament, the contrast between flesh and spirit is a contrast between two substances, one heavy and gross, the other light and pure: it is a different kind of contrast from that which is attempted to be conceived in modern times, the contrast between 'matter', i.e. something which is subject to what are called 'laws of nature', and 'spirit' which is thought of as altogether non-material.

73

To go into all the details of the fantastic cosmo-gony set forth in the Three Books of *Pistis Sophia*, and in the Anonymous work which follows it, would be both confusing and fatiguing, all the more as the main principles are everywhere the same. There is the same parade of ever fresh and more powerful 'mysteries', which Schmidt so rightly takes as a sign of decadence. 'The greatest care is directed towards obtaining the highest place in the realms of Light by means of the Mysteries. The former simple Mysteries are no longer enough, and so in later times new Mysteries are invented' (*Pistis Sophia*, p. liii). With unwearied diligence Prof. Schmidt has made out the genealogy of our documents. According to him the Three Books of *Pistis Sophia* are later than the Anonymous work at the end of the Askew MS, and this in turn is later than the Two Books of Jeū in the Bruce Papyrus.

At the same time there is nothing really fresh. The 'First Mystery' really contains everything. In *Pistis Sophia* 198 ff. there is a sort of crescendo of 'mysteries', there is the 'first-mystery' and the mystery of the first Thrice-spiritual, and of the second, and of the third, and finally we get to the absolute authentic Mystery of the First Mystery of the Ineffable (*Pistis Sophia* 205), which is so exalted that the Disciples lose courage when they hear about it and only Mary Magdalene dares question Jesus further—then Jesus explains that this is the easiest of all mysteries (*Pistis Sophia* 218), about which He had said aforetime, 'Come unto Me all ye that are heavy under your burden, and I will refresh you'. And He adds, 'Amen, I say to you, that mystery is yours and every one's who will renounce the whole world and all the matter therein'. It is in fact 'the only word of the Ineffable' (226).

But what is this glorious mystery? The Jesus of the *Pistis Sophia* makes it quite clear to the Disciples: it is Himself. 'That mystery is I, and I am that mystery' (231): 'I am the knowledge of the universe' (233). In other words, what is 'necessary to everlasting salvation' is that one shall 'believe rightly the Incarnation of our Lord Jesus Christ'. We have travelled by another route, but we have arrived at the end at something very much like the Athanasian Creed! And, as I pointed out at the beginning of these Lectures,[1] the Gnostic believed that in the full apprehension of the place and nature of Jesus in the Universe all other mysteries would resolve themselves. As I said, 'the knowledge of the true nature of Divine things seems to the initiate to make everything clear'. Our Copt, with truly Egyptian and un-Hellenic particularity, enumerates the mysteries of the universe in detail. The mystery of Jesus will explain why there is darkness and light, why the impious and the good, why cursing and blessing. And the eighty-nine distinctions (206–16) which this great mystery will explain are not confined to generali-

[1] P. 6.

ties. It will explain the winds and famines and the cause of matter and the nature of metals, and (most curious of all) 'why the matter of glass has arisen and why the matter of wax has arisen'. Here, at least, we have the thought of some one who has been struck with the curious diversity of the things we see and touch. Glass is hard and impenetrable, but you can see through it; wax, on the other hand, is soft but opaque. It is interesting to know that our Copt felt the anomaly, and also that he hoped it would be resolved when he really understood his Master!

The attainment of this high state of insight demands, according to the doctrine of the book *Pistis Sophia*, the renunciation of all worldly aims. The Disciples are to teach the whole world to seek the mysteries of the Light which will purify them and make them refined light, but to attain this men must renounce the whole world and the matter therein and all its cares and sins and associations (255). What this means in detail is explained in a list of some thirty sins—cursing, thieving, robbery, adultery, etc.—while on the other hand almsgiving, gentleness, a loving disposition to GOD and man, are to be enjoined: to such the Gnostic mysteries may be imparted, so that their sins may be forgiven and they may be received into the Kingdom of Light. There were other Gnostic sects that were given to evil practices (cf. *Pistis Sophia* 387), but our documents are moral even to asceticism.

And the reward of the true Gnostic, who has

reached true insight, what is it? It is that when he or she is set free from the body of matter such a soul becomes a great light-stream or ray, which cannot be seized by the intermediate Archons and rulers of the lower heavens, it does not need to produce passports or tokens, but passes direct through all the regions and goes to the region where it belongs, that of the One Ineffable, and becomes a part of the Ineffable itself: 'Amen, I say to you', adds Jesus to the Disciples, 'it will be in all the regions in the time a man takes to shoot an arrow' (228). Such a man, He adds, is a man in the world, but in reality he is above all archangels and even above the various dignitaries of the heavenly hierarchy. 'He is a man in the world, but he is king in the Light. He is a man in the world, but he is not one of the world,—and Amen, I say to you, that man is I and I am that man' (230). Not, however, entirely: on the next page we learn that though all these truly enlightened ones will be fellow kings with Jesus in His kingdom, Mary Magdalene and John the virgin will be on Jesus' right and left, and the throne of Jesus will be highest of all. It is remarkable what respect the writer of *Pistis Sophia* has for the women-disciples: is it not possible that the writer was a woman?

GOD TROUBLING HIMSELF ABOUT MAN

One or two detached points here deserve notice. I have mentioned in Chapter II the use in Coptic of the word ⲥⲕⲩⲗⲗⲓ ⲙ̄ⲙⲟⲓ (for σκύλλεσθαι).[1] It is worth while to examine the context (248 f.). After hearing the great privileges and dignity of the perfect initiate, Andrew asks how men who are in the world and wrapped in matter can pass through the regions of the celestial Archons and take their place above them? To this Jesus answers that all these Heavenly Powers are of the same nature and stuff as the souls of men: these Powers are indeed shining and glorious, but that is part of the arrangements made by Providence, they themselves have not troubled themselves in the matter. But men—at least, some men—though lower in the scale, the mere dregs of Light, have struggled towards a better state, they have not left off seeking, and therefore Jesus for the sake of the race of men *troubled Himself* (σκύλλεσθαι) to come down and teach the saving Mysteries.

Well, that is the Christian doctrine. The pagan doctrine, whether true or false, taught that visible matter is the great evil and that the human body is the prison or tomb of an ethereal spirit, and this pagan doctrine at least agreed with the New Testament doctrine that man was in an evil case. But it is the peculiarly Christian doctrine that GOD was not only sorry for man, but troubled Himself to come down to earth to give man the help he needed. The language of *Pistis Sophia* is different from the language of Paul and of John, corresponding to the difference between the view of

[1] P. 41.

the Cosmos, visible and invisible, pictured by the Egyptian Gnostic and the early Christian writers respectively. But it seems to me that they have very much the same theology, and that they give the same place in the great scheme of Things to the career of 'Jesus who appeared in Judaea'.[1] Or, to put the matter from another point of view, these Gnostic systems, even the fantastic mythology of *Pistis Sophia*, do not exhibit a self-sufficient philosophy, but an attempt to reformulate the Christian Religion in terms of what was then more or less current Astronomy and Physics. What makes it so strange and fantastic to us is that the astronomy and physics assumed in *Pistis Sophia* are so much more out-of-date than its religious faith.

'MAMMON'

Another matter, which seems somehow to have escaped attention, is the significance of the reference to the text about making a friend out of the mammon of unrighteousness (Lk. xvi 9). This text is quoted in *Pistis Sophia* 334 f. Jesus had been asked what the fate is of one who has been initiated and then become careless, when he dies and is engulfed in the Dragon of the Outer Darkness. He answers that such an one, if he does but know one of the twelve names of the Dragon, will escape out of torment and be received in the treasury of souls, though in the lowest place. Mary then answers that this is what Jesus had said aforetime

[1] Mani's phrase: see my *Religion of the Manichees*, p. 38.

in a similitude (i.e. in the Gospels), and adds, 'Who then is the *Mamōn* of unrighteousness, if not the Dragon of the outer darkness?'

I venture to think this fantastic piece of exegesis is not the work of the Coptic compiler of *Pistis Sophia*, but goes back to the second-century adversaries of Irenaeus. Irenaeus, having set forth the Gnostic doctrines in his first Book against Heresies, having pointed out their weaknesses and inconsistencies in his second, goes on in his third Book to set forth the true Catholic faith founded on the Four Gospels which are alone received at Rome, a church whose leaders descend in unbroken succession from S. Peter and S. Paul. He backs this up by the general consent of the Christian world, and shews that the Scriptures know of no other GOD but the Father of all and His Word. This takes up the first six chapters, and though some of the argumentation may be fanciful it is a continuous and reasoned theory. But before Irenaeus goes on to examine the theology of the Four Gospels he thinks it well to explain away Paul's odd phrase in 2 Cor. iv 4 about 'the God of this world', a phrase which does give a handle to any one who might hold that the true GOD was not the immediate author of this world—and then proceeds to explain 'Mammon' (Iren. *Haer.* III 8). It comes in oddly: one may well wonder why Irenaeus pauses in his argument to explain that Mammon is not a Divine Name. But if it was already used by his opponents as the name equivalent almost to the Lord of Hell the explanation, confused as it is, is not out of place.

ABERAMENTHŌ(U)

The Anonymous treatise at the end of the Askew MS (*Pistis Sophia* 357–90)[1] is a separate work from the Three Books of *Pistis Sophia* which precede it, with a separate independent Introduction. In C. Schmidt's opinion, which appears to be well founded, it is earlier than *Pistis Sophia*, but comes from much the same Gnostic circles. What is special in it is a more definite Astrology. The 'Sphere', i.e. the visible heavens, and its rulers are described, the chariot of the Sun, the ship of the Moon, and the five Planets (with their 'incorruptible', i.e. fanciful, names). Further we are told of five aërial Demons, one of whom has the Greek name Hecate, which seize the souls of sinners after their death and torment them. But the particular point of this whole revelation, put like the rest of the contents of *Pistis Sophia* into the mouth of the risen Jesus, is to explain that Jesus in mercy has arranged that the several classes of sinners are released from their torments whenever certain astronomical conjunctions occur. For instance, when Jupiter is in Scorpio and at the same time Venus is in Taurus, then all the souls which have been tormented by Hecate for over 105 years are released and (apparently) given a new chance (368 f.). In other

[1] Schmidt, pp. 261–85; Mead, 5th and 6th Books, pp. 295–325.

words, what is described is a kindly arrangement made to shorten the sufferings of those in Hell.

Three times in this section, and nowhere else in the book, or indeed in Christian Gnostic literature so far as I am aware, Jesus is called *Aberamenthō* (358, 365, 373).[1] The phrase used in each case is 'Jesus, i.e. Aberamenthō, said...'. The obvious deduction is that the saga or legend belongs to 'Aberamenthō' (whoever he may be), but has been transferred, perhaps with modifications, to the gnostic Jesus.

What is the derivation of Aberamenthō? Where else does this curious name occur? With regard to the first question it may be remarked that it does not look like Coptic or Hebrew or Aramaic or Iranian. The only other place I have come across it is a magic invocation in what is known as the Leiden Papyrus.[2] This invocation is a very curious formula, transcribed in Greek in a non-Christian Demotic (i.e. Egyptian) work, which seems to have been written a little before or after A.D. 200. The invocation is of Typhon,—he is called *Typhon Sēth*, a double name like *Pistis Sophia*,—who is conjured to strike down so-and-so with frost and fire. He is invoked by his 'authentic' name, in terms which he cannot refuse to hear. These are: 'Iō erbēth, Iō pakerbēth, Iō bolchōsēth, Iō pata-

---

[1] The occurrence in 373 is just outside the astronomical section. I fancy it has been introduced by the final editor, to join it up with what precedes.

[2] F. Ll. Griffith and Herbert Thompson, *The Demotic Magical Papyrus of London and Leiden*, 3 vols. (London, 1904).

thanax, Iō sōrō, Iō nebutosualēth, Aktiōphi Ereschi-
gal Nebuposoalēth, Aberamenthōu, Lerthexanax,
Ethrelyōth, Nemareba, Aemina'.[1]

This is not all gibberish, though some of it may
be. *Eresh-ki-gal* is the old Sumerian Goddess of
the Underworld, and the formula ⲁⲭⲣⲓⲟ︢ϥⲓ ⲉⲣⲉⲭⲓⲅⲁⲅ
ⲛⲉⲃⲟⲩⲧⲓⲥⲟⲧⲁⲗⲏⲟ, i.e. the same as in the Papyrus
except for a couple of mistakes, occurs on a gem.[2]
The inventor of the curse has clearly collected
foreign, that is to say non-Egyptian, Names for
the Lord of the Underworld, not always correctly
spelt. May not therefore ⲁⲃⲉⲣⲁⲙⲉⲛⲑⲱⲟⲩ be a deformation of 'Rhadamanthus'? In Aeolic ῾Ραδά-
μανθυσ is spelt ΒΡΑΔΑΜΑΝΘΥϹ. If the medial δ
between two α's was dropped or misread, something very much like *Aberamentho* is the result. A
culture that produced Ialdabaoth and Iabraoth
might easily produce such a form. Rhadamanthus
in Classical tradition was just and kindly, as is the
Aberamentho of *Pistis Sophia*.

THE BOOKS OF JEU (᾿Ιεοῦ)

The first part of the Bruce Papyrus, edited by C.
Schmidt in *Texte und Untersuchungen*, vol. VIII,[3] is a
very queer document. But Prof. Schmidt has
thrown some light upon the jungle,[4] and we can
follow with confidence the trail he has blazed out.

[1] Transl. p. 147.
[2] C. W. King, *The Gnostics and their Remains*, p. 318.
[3] *Gnostische Schriften* (T. und U. VIII 1, 2): see above,
p. 63.
[4] Schmidt, *Pistis Sophia*, p. lxxxi.

I venture to think that he is right in identifying the Two Books of Ieu mentioned in *Pistis Sophia* (245, 354) with the Two Books of the 'Great Mystery-treatise of Jeu', i.e. the work in the Bruce Papyrus, so that it is older than *Pistis Sophia* itself.

We are still in the same situation as in most of these 'gnostic' revelations: Jesus is revealing the higher mysteries to His Disciples after His resurrection. The main subject this time appears to be Cosmogony. We are introduced to Ieu (ιεου), 'the God of truth', whose special Name is Ioeiaōthō-uikhōlmiō. He is not the ultimate Unapproachable GOD, but an emanation. It was Ieu's duty to praise this ultimate GOD, Whom Jesus calls His Father, but apparently had no power to do so. So 'a little thought' was sent from the Father of Jesus into the 'God of truth', and this gave him the energy to utter from himself, saying *ie ie ie*. It does not seem very much, but it was sufficient—enough to build the Cosmos with! The poor little syllables (as I understand the story) came from Ieu, not from the ultimate GOD. It was something fresh, something distinct. Where there had been only the One and its direct emanations, there was now Two.

After this we read how the 'God of truth' evolved out of himself sixty emanations, all called Ieu, and we are given their signs and seals: one might call the diagrams their several family armorial bearings.[1] Further, there are the sixty

[1] That of the original Ieu, 'the Father of all Ieus', has three strokes in it, to represent the three original noises!

Treasuries of the Light-world, over which those who follow Jesus and receive His Mysteries have power, and there is a long Hymn of Praise chanted by Jesus to the Ultimate unapproachable GOD, to every clause of which the Disciples respond with 'Amen, amen, amen'. There is an incredible amount of verbiage and repetition, but the only real action is the three impulsive cries of the first Ieu.

I feel that the author of this strange book has deluded himself, and wishes to delude his readers, into thinking that he has really explained how multiplicity came out of unity, how heterogeneity came out of undifferentiated uniformity, how shade came out of light. I think he understood by Ieu's *ie ie ie* a sound which was so unformed that it needed no lungs, no mouth, no organs, *uox et praeterea nihil*. But once these sounds were made they could be magnified and strengthened, like the Hertzian waves in a loud speaker! In other words, our author was one of that numerous tribe of human beings who believe in their hearts that you can propel a boat in which you are sitting by pressing against the sides (if you only knew the trick)! What a good thing it was for Christian thought that this account of ultimate origins did not become canonical!

You have probably had enough of Gnostic Cosmogony by this time. But I cannot take leave of the subject without a guess—it is no more—at the origin of the name ʼΙεοῦ, and of the sounds *ie ie ie*. The 'God of truth' suggests the Old Testament: it is actually an Old Testament expression (Psalm xxx 6), and the God of the Jews was, at least to some Gnostics, a real but inferior Deity. We have further to consider the name ιεογ itself: what is its relation to ιαω, a form attested by Gnostic gems, as well as by *Pistis Sophia* 358? ιαω does seem to have been the traditional pronunciation of the Tetragrammaton. But if the real pronunciation was in some sense a mystery, at least the spelling could be known. I cannot help feeling that ιεογ is a sort of transcription of יהו and that ιε is הי.

In any case the 'praise' offered to the ultimate, unapproachable GOD by the 'God of truth', though it consisted only in the utterance of the syllables *ie ie ie*, is the only thing that really happens in the Books of Ieu: the rest, like the paraphrases of Psalms uttered by *Pistis Sophia*, is nothing more than a measure of the poverty of imagination exhibited by Coptic-speaking Gnostics.

BASILIDES AND ABRASAX

I ought perhaps to have found more room in this survey for the curious speculations of Basilides. A good deal of obscurity hangs over them and over the subsequent history of his followers. But one point may be noticed here. Prominent in his hierarchy was the Archon Abrasax (also called Abraxas), ruler of one of the Heavens, of which in the Basilidean system there were 365: it will be noticed that the letters of Abrasax, when added together, come to 365. The point of the 365 heavens was that each was less concrete, less material, than the one below it, till at last in the ultimate region we arrive at what is altogether Nothing![1] This does not seem to me a very helpful presentation; I confess to preferring the Valentinian Notion which welled up out of the immeasurable Deep, or even the 'little thought' which entered into the helpless 'God of truth' and stirred him up to uttering his three monosyllabic but epoch-making cries! The fact is we do not know how diversity can come out of unity, or the concrete out of the undifferentiated, any more than we know the real nature of our own consciousness of ourselves and of other things. The 365 heavens of Basilides appear to me to be nothing more than an attempt to acquit the ultimate Heavenly Power of responsibility for letting this material concrete world come into existence.

It is time to sum up now the main thoughts about the 'Gnostics' and their speculations which I have attempted to put before you. It is the old traditional view, with a difference. I regard the Gnostic systems, from Valentinus to *Pistis Sophia*, as essentially Christian systems, though doubtless heretical. The foreign element in these systems is not a non-Christian 'gnosis' or philosophy, more or less self-consistent, but with a few Christian

[1] Hippolytus, *Haer.* VII 20.

elements (such as the figure of the gnostic 'Jesus') superadded. On the contrary, the figure of Jesus is essential, and without Jesus the systems would drop to pieces. In my view the systems were invented to explain Jesus in terms of the science of the day by Christians who were dissatisfied with the Old Testament, or rather with that view of GOD and the Universe, which the Old Testament seems to set forth. That the Old Testament and the Christian Gospels were Books of Mystery, containing hints of the profoundest philosophy and cosmogony the Gnostics for the most part were willing and eager to believe. But they could not accept them as they stood, because as they stood the statements of the Scriptures were in opposition to the main conclusions of the science and philosophy current in the Graeco-Roman civilization. These conclusions were chiefly embodied in the Ptolemaic Astronomy and the belief in the natural immortality of the human soul. The former of these led directly to the doctrine of the celestial spheres and to astrology with its accompaniment of planetary Fate, while the latter doctrine had as its rider the notion that the material body was a prison to the ethereal soul within it. Gnosticism appears to me to be an attempt to combine these ideas with Christianity, and I mean in this connexion by 'Christianity' a conviction that 'Jesus who appeared in Judaea' in the days of Pontius Pilate had been an authoritative mission from the ultimate, unapproachable GOD, sent of His own

free will to enlighten those who would follow Him
and to deliver their immortal part after their bodily
death from being cast back into the miseries of
this sinful world.

It may be objected to this view that the gnostic
Jesus does not seem to have an entirely intelligible
status in the gnostic hierarchy. No, indeed: how
should He? It is the same in the religion of Mani.
But that is only another way of saying that Gnosticism is not a really satisfactory religious theory.
The Jewish Prophet, more than a Prophet perhaps,
who had had a brief but tragic career among the
Jews, was very much unlike Hermes Trismegistos,
in whom we really do see embodied the contemporary notion of what a Divine Teacher ought to
have been. In the system of Valentinus we do see
indeed some attempt to represent Jesus as one in
whom all the fulness (or *pleroma*) of the complicated Divine Nature dwelt, an idea directly taken
from S. Paul;[1] but when (as in *Pistis Sophia* and the
Books of Ieu) we hear the Gnostic speaking for
himself we find Jesus occupying an altogether
peculiar position in the heavenly hierarchy. He is
at once more real and more mysterious than the
other personages and powers. On the one hand
He is the authoritative Mystagogue; He reveals and
performs the highest sacramental, miraculous,
rites. He passes through the heavenly regions and
all do Him obeisance. As in the Gospel, He speaks
of His Father and certainly means by that term the

[1] Colossians i 19, ii 9.

ultimate GOD. But He reveals to the Disciples the grandiose fabric of the Universe, both material and ethereal, with its Archons and Regions and Treasuries of the Light—what is *His* place in it? That is never explained.

My point is that this was inevitable, because the Gnostics were, in the last resort, Christians and had no 'explanation' for Jesus. He remained more real to them as a 'Saviour' than the fantastic demonic organization from which they understood that He was saving them. But their permanent merit did not lie in inventing a theory of religion which should, so to speak, put Jesus Christ into His proper place. Their merit was in recognizing that some new theory of religion was called for. The special constructions of Valentinus and Basilides and their rivals were rejected by the Great Church, and the speculations of these thoughtful men were driven into holes and corners of the Christian world, where they became the foundation of a crude mythology such as we find in the Coptic works discussed in this chapter. But by the time the struggle was over what is called 'Chiliasm' had begun to fade into the background of the Christian consciousness. In the East the Apocalypse of John was already dropping out of favour, and documents such as the Apocalypse of Peter began to take its place, documents in which attention was concentrated on the state of good and bad souls immediately after death, rather than on a general resurrection at an anticipated return of

Christ to earth with attendant rewards and punishments.

It was a difference of emphasis rather than a repudiation of old beliefs, but the new emphasis fitted better with the ideas of the Graeco-Roman world, and removed a stumbling-block in the way of the conversion of the thoughtful classes. In any case I venture to think that we ought to see in the so-called 'Gnostic' systems of the second century mainly an attempt to set forth what a generation ago used to be called 'the new theology': that is to say, a reformulation of Christianity in terms of 'modern' science and philosophy. The science of that time was crude and the philosophy too greatly belittled the things of sense, so that the Gnostic 'new theology' was unsatisfactory. Perhaps the safest moral that can be drawn is the danger of lightly abandoning the Past at the bidding of present-day ideas. All the same, the dangerous renunciation has to be attempted from time to time.

Chapter IV

THE FOURTH GOSPEL: MANDAISM
AND CHRISTIANITY

IT is time now to give some account of the Mandaean Religion. One of the most curious developments of theological criticism in the last few years is the attention paid to the Mandaeans of Iraq: it has even been alleged that the Fourth Gospel shews signs of having been originally intended as a sacred book of a sect akin to these Mandaeans, and that what we have is a revision made to turn it into a Christian work. I shall venture to pass over this paradoxical theory here, because even if true it would not cease to be extremely paradoxical. The Mandaean sacred Books were not gathered together till after the victories of Islam: it would be indeed surprising if they demonstrably set forth a religious theory of which the Gospel according to John, a work published in its present form about the end of the first Christian century, presented a later development! In fact it seems to me that the theory could only have been entertained by learned men at all because the current theory of the meaning of the Fourth Gospel had been felt to be in some respects unsatisfactory. I propose therefore to begin by considering the opening section of this Gospel itself.

But first let me make a distinction between the

actual teaching of the Fourth Gospel and what is commonly spoken of as 'the Logos-doctrine'. We are often invited to regard the Word or Logos spoken of in the opening sentences of the Gospel as identical with the Logos expounded by Philo, the Alexandrian Jewish philosopher. The Evangelist goes on to assert that this Logos became flesh, which was a step beyond the conceptions of Philo; but we are invited to read into the word *Logos*, used by the Evangelist, all or most of the Philonean notions, which in turn are ultimately derived from Plato. These notions were very attractive to many Christians, from the second century onwards, among others to Justin Martyr, who has much to say about the Logos, though indeed he makes curiously little direct use of the Fourth Gospel, if he derived his Logos-doctrine from it. At any rate, from the time of Justin Martyr onwards, the Logos of the Gospel has been generally regarded as the Philonean, Platonic, *logos*.

Now in the first place one must remark that *logos*, λόγοσ, is one of the commonest words in the Greek language. It means of course a word, a discourse, an account (both in the sense of 'narrative' and of 'bill'),[1] and also reason and plan. We should be wary of assigning a special technical sense to such a term, unless the usage of the writer is established. And in the Fourth Gospel itself we have a notable instance, as everybody will remember, where 'the Word of GOD' is not used of

[1] E.g. Lk. xvi 2.

Jesus at all, but corresponds rather with the inspiration usually ascribed in New Testament language to the 'Spirit'. If 'the Logos' has been a technical term to the Fourth Evangelist it is almost impossible to understand how he could have worded, as he has done, the argument that the Scripture called Gods those to whom 'the word of GOD' came (Joh. x 34–6).

We must therefore not assume that λόγοσ, 'word', in the opening sentences of the Fourth Gospel necessarily means the Philonean Logos. Let us then turn to the phrases themselves and see whether they do not explain their own meaning. 'In the Beginning was the Word', ἐν ἀρχῇ ἦν ὁ λόγοσ—one thing at least is certain about this sentence. No one could begin a work with ἐν ἀρχῇ without at once carrying back his Christian or Jewish readers to the first words of Genesis. To begin a work in this way practically means 'I am starting where Genesis starts, what I say is what Genesis says in other words'. Well then, what was the 'word' that was there in the Beginning? I think we know it very well, it was Γενηθήτω φῶσ, 'Let there be light'. And that this is correct is confirmed by the way that the Evangelist immediately goes on to talk about Light, and how it shined in Darkness.

But this word or sentence or decree—to whom was it spoken? Not to 'light', for light did not yet exist. Nothing yet existed, nothing yet had happened, the 'word' had been in the beginning, before things happened. There was nothing, no one, to whom it could be spoken but GOD. The word had been addressed to GOD.[1] The alternative translation, that the word was *with* GOD (*apud Deum*) seems to me unsatisfactory, for as used elsewhere εἶναι πρόσ τινα conveys the idea of mere juxtaposition, not of intimate genetic connexion.

'What', do you say, 'a word addressed to GOD? Who by?' So the Evangelist, anticipating the objection, adds καὶ θεὸσ ἦν ὁ λόγοσ, 'and the Word was itself Divine'. What the Evangelist introduces us to is no new theology, but the familiar, though lofty, conception of Genesis, viz. that of the One only GOD producing the creation by consulting with Himself, yet bringing forth into visible form nothing without announcing His formulated intention.[2] What had come to pass in consequence of this intention was Life. Light as distinct from darkness was the most general feature of existence, but in the case of Man this 'light' was best called Life.

Further, this Word or Intention 'was' (ἦν), whereas 'all things came to pass' (ἐγένετο) through it. The difference between these verbs is not ontological, the difference is simply that the Word, so to speak, is on the stage when the curtain goes

[1] πρόσ τὸν θεόν. So also Joh. x 35, π ρ ὸ σ οὖσ ὁ λόγοσ τοῦ θεοῦ ἐγένετο, and Jeremiah xiv 1, etc.

[2] Compare also Amos iii 7. If we are to use Valentinian phraseology we might say that the visible universe was no haphazard happening, but was brought forth by Wisdom (σοφία) in accordance with design (θελητόσ).

up, while the 'things' are not. 'There was (ἦν) a man in Babylon' at the beginning of *Susanna*, 'There was (ἦν) a man of Mount Ephraim' at the beginning of *Samuel*, 'There was (ἦν) a man in the region of Ausitis' at the beginning of *Job*. We are not to infer that Job or the father of Samuel or the husband of Susanna existed from eternity; all the word implies is that each is on the scene when the action begins. Similarly, in the first verse of the Fourth Gospel the Word of GOD is postulated, it was there at the beginning, and to inquire whether ἦν ποτε, ὅτε οὐκ ἦν, whether there was anything before that, is to look outside the frame for the rest of the picture.

Then, in the sixth verse of the Gospel, a certain John is introduced to us: a man divinely commissioned to bear witness about the divine Light, not that John himself was this Light, for the true Light was there just then, coming into the world, though unknown and unrecognized.[1] But to those who did receive Him, says the Evangelist, He gave fresh supplies of power, power to become children of GOD by a new and non-material process. 'I mean to say', he continues, 'the Word itself became human and we saw Him': as far as I can see, the καὶ of καὶ ὁ λόγοσ σάρξ ἐγένετο is resumptive,

[1] I take ἐρχόμενον (*ver.* 9) to be a nominative, agreeing with φῶσ, not as an accusative agreeing with πάντα ἄνθρωπον. This interpretation has left a trace in Cyprian, *Test.* i 7 (*ueniens in hunc mundum*, L* (*sic*) MO_1 O_3 $P\underline{Q}V$ and *Cass*: all other Latins have *uenientem*). Human beings when they 'come into the world' have very little but animal life.

and should be translated by 'I mean to say' or 'Well, then', not by 'And'.[1] The Evangelist then goes back to John, whom he had introduced to his readers already, and gives John's testimony about the one who was to come, passing on (after his usual careless manner of writing) to words of his own (*vv.* 16–18), which sum up the Prologue. These words seem to me to be a summary in other terms of what has been already said, not to announce a fresh development.

It is most important to note how far we have got, to what point the narrative of the Gospel has arrived. As I understand the matter, the readers of the Gospel have been introduced to John; they have also been told something about a mysterious personage called Jesus Christ, but they have not yet been introduced to Him. An introduction is clearly necessary, for we have been told that the 'world' knew Him not and that His own did not receive Him. So the Evangelist goes on to tell us in detail what the testimony of John was. It was, in the first place, an emphatic denial that he, John, was the Christ or Elijah or 'the Prophet', but he declared that he was the prophetic Voice preparing the way, come to make known who the mysterious Coming One was. Then one day, when he sees Jesus coming up, he says, 'There is the Lamb of GOD!' How does he know? He tells us that he

[1] For this use of καί, see especially *Timothy and Aquila*, p. 76, and my Note on that passage in *Evangelion da-Mepharreshe*, II 265.

had learned by inspiration that the one on whom he saw the Spirit of GOD descending like a dove was He who would baptize with holy Spirit: he had seen the Spirit descending upon Jesus, and so he testifies that Jesus is the Chosen of GOD (ὁ ἐκλεκτὸσ τοῦ θεοῦ).[1]

Now the secret is out, so to speak; in fact, more than one secret. First of all, we see the rôle of John according to the Fourth Evangelist. John is the witness of the Incarnation! It is he who introduces us to Jesus, to Jesus as the Messiah.

I cannot resist the impression that the doctrine of the Fourth Gospel is what is usually called 'adoptionist', and that we do wrong to combine its presentation with the Infancy Narratives of Matthew and Luke. As I understand the tale told in the first chapter of John, what is taught in that chapter is that the creative word of GOD, which had of old produced light and energy out of nothing, descended upon the man Jesus and remained upon him; John actually witnessed this event and had been inspired to know its meaning. The Fourth Gospel does not say that John baptized Jesus, but that he witnessed the descent of the Spirit of GOD: that descent, as I understand the text, *was* the Incarnation. After the descent of the Spirit, witnessed by John, Jesus (hitherto called son of Joseph, Joh. i 45, vi 42) became the incarnate word

---

[1] Joh. i 34 ℵ* *e ff* syr.sc. There can be little doubt that this is the true reading here.

of GOD, born from above not by natural process but by the Divine will.

This is not orthodox Christology, but it does seem to me to be Johannine Christology. It explains why the Evangelist is so careful to introduce his readers to the 'man sent from GOD whose name was John', for this man in his turn will introduce us to the incarnate Jesus Christ, rightly called from the moment of His incarnation the Lamb of GOD. The only reason that it has not been obvious to all readers of the Fourth Gospel is the tacit assumption that whatever its authorship or date may turn out to be that Gospel must be regarded as strictly orthodox in doctrine. I venture to think, on the other hand, that at the end of the first century A.D. there was not yet any 'orthodox' Christology, that Christians were feeling after a Christology, a doctrine about the personality of Jesus their Lord, and that a synthesis had not yet been reached. Whether the belief in the Virgin Birth of Jesus was accepted by the Fourth Evangelist, whether even he had heard of it, we do not know. But I think his silence about it leads us to suppose that he attached very little importance to the matter. What mattered to him was the real Descent of the Spirit, and that it had not been given to Jesus by measure but fully.

From the moment of the Descent Jesus can say 'I and the Father are one' (ἕν ἐσμεν, x 30: cf. I Cor. iii 8): what He says is creative and authoritative, because it is of the same nature as the Divine Voice of which we read in the opening chapter of Genesis. In the terminology of *Pistis Sophia*, Jesus has become the Master of the ineffable Mystery: 'He is a man in the world, but He towereth above all angels and will tower still more above them all; He is a man in the world, but He is King in the Light'.[1] And, just as in *Pistis Sophia*, the true Life consists in knowing Him.

THE MANDAEANS

Those who accept the explanation given above of the appearance of John the Baptist's name in the opening verses of the Fourth Gospel will not, I think, feel it necessary to regard that work as a Christianized version of a Gospel about John. But so much has been written in late years about the Mandaeans and their connexion with the Baptist, that some account of them here will not be out of place. They have at least this interest, that whatever their remote origin may have been, they are certainly the only surviving Gnostic Sect.

The Mandaeans are a religious community still to be found in Lower Babylonia, on the lower reaches of the Tigris and the Euphrates. The very frequent ablutions required by their religion make residence on or near the bank of a flowing river necessary for them. They call themselves Mandaeans, which really does mean 'Gnostics', but they are locally known as *Ṣubbis*, i.e. baptizers. Their

[1] *Pistis Sophia* 228 ff.

sacred Book is called the *Ginza*, i.e. the Treasure. Another, of miscellaneous contents, is known as the Book of John (or, of the Kings). There is also a sort of Hymn-book, called *Qolasta*. These are all written in an Aramaic dialect, akin to Syriac. The Mandaean script is peculiar: the gutturals א and ע have disappeared and ה and ח have become simple *h*,[1] but the guttural letters are used for vowels, א for *a*, ע for *e*, besides the usual Aramaic use of ו for *o* and *u*, and of י for *i*. The sacred Book, the *Ginza*, is divided into two parts, that concerned with the Living and that concerned with the Dead: these are always bound up, so that each begins the book, but from opposite ends, meeting in the middle; the one part is upside down to the other, just like a Note-Book which has been begun at both ends. The two parts are known respectively as the Right and the Left *Ginza*.

How are we to class these people? It is rather important to take hold of them properly, so to speak. When Roman Catholic missionaries first came across them in the seventeenth century they conjectured that the Mandaeans were descended from disciples of John the Baptist, such as are mentioned in Acts xviii 25 ff., and so these missionaries named them 'Christians of S. John'. This erroneous idea is now universally abandoned, but it survives in an altered form, and there are still those who regard the Mandaeans as the survivors of a Palestinian sect or school.

[1] Occasionally ע is represented by *h* as in *rkiha* = ܪܩܝܚܐ.

We have now, in the *Scholion* of Theodore bar Konai (or Kēwāni), an account of the Mandaeans by an ancient Mesopotamian writer,[1] writing in the year A.D. 792. He tells us that their founder was a certain Ado, a mendicant, who came from Adiabene, i.e. from the district just north of Mosul. He further tells us that his teaching was derived from the Marcionites, from the Manichaeans and from the 'Kanteans'. These latter are only known from Theodore himself: it is very possible that the name should be vocalized *Knāthāyē*, which might mean something like 'the Colleagues'.

There is no reason to reject the evidence of Theodore bar Konai. He was writing about a century after the *Ginza* had been compiled, for the *Ginza* (G.R. 387) expects the end of the Arab dominion after 71 years, i.e. a little after A.D. 700. But of course the matter does not end here. It is important to consider how much his evidence comes to. There *is* a good deal in the Mandaean literature that recalls Marcionite and Manichaean teaching, especially as set forth in the polemics of S. Ephraim against these religions. Who were the *Knāthāyē*? Our authority, Theodore, gives a clearly fantastic account of them, asserting that they were Babylonian descendants of Philistine priests of Dagon[2]. I think we may judge from this that they were not recognizably a Christian or Jewish sect,

[1] See H. Pognon, *Coupes de Khouabir* (1898), esp. pp. 224-7.
[2] Pognon, p. 151.

and this corresponds with the fact that there is in the Mandaean mythology a large element which is neither Biblical nor Christian, e.g. that connected with Ptahil and Abatur. We may therefore paraphrase Theodore's account of the Mandaeans by saying that this religion is a mixture of Christian and non-Christian elements, the Christian elements being mostly derived from Marcionite and Manichaean sources.

But even so our problem is not solved. Before we reject the idea, so popular in Germany of late years, that the Mandaean documents throw valuable side-lights on the earliest Christian traditions, we must get some positive idea of what the Mandaean religion really is. How shall we interrogate the vast and miscellaneous Mandaean literature, so as to make it answer our questions?

I think we should begin with what is called the Left-hand *Ginza*, the part concerned with the Dead. In G.L. 82 f. (= III 8) we read that when the soul of the good Mandaean departs there is confusion in *Tibil*, i.e. the material world, and its Rulers gather together and say:

Who has taken away the Pearl: that illuminated the falling house?

In the house that it has left: the walls cracked and fell in.

Its walls cracked and fell in: and its door-posts fell to the ground.

Its windows were shut: and its lamps quenched and shone not.

[The Soul speaks:]

Mine eyes see no more: what is done in the present age.

Mine ears hear no more: what is said in the present age.

My feet tread no more: in the present age, nor do they
    return.
The soul that is worthy speaks and goes away: from the
    world even unto the abode of light.[1]
Naked was I brought into the world: and empty am I come
    out of it.
Empty am I come out of it: like a bird that carries no load.
My reward goes on in front: and my alms follow behind.
The Waterwaves I hold in my hand: and turn my course to
    the abode of light.

The 'Waterwaves' are the power of the cleans-
ing waters of Mandaean baptisms.

When the Seven, i.e. the hostile Planets, see the
soul they try to arrest its course, but fail, and they
ask:

With whose power hast thou come forth: and whose Name
    has been spoken over thee?—
I have come forth with the power of Life: and the Name of
    the chief of Brightness has been spoken over me;
The Waterwaves I hold in my hand: and turn my course to
    the abode of light.

Here you have in poetic form the essence of
Mandaism. The poetic form consists chiefly of a
skilful use of repetition, very much as in Babylonian style, but something like it is to be seen in
the prose homilies of Narsai the Nestorian Doctor
(fl. A.D. 500). *Tibil* is used for the material world:
this is the Hebrew תֵּבֵל, but it should be noticed
that this word is transliterated from the Hebrew
in the form ܬܒܝܠ also in the Syriac Bible. As for
the doctrine, it is clearly 'Gnostic', dominated by
the *soma-sema* view of human life, and by a belief

[1] *Sic.*

in baleful astrological Fate. This world is bad; the soul of man has its true home elsewhere, but apart from its possession of the true knowledge it cannot escape through the Spheres and is liable to be cast back again into a human body!

This is the doctrine of *Pistis Sophia* also, and of Gnostic systems generally. But, as I pointed out in the beginning of these Lectures, it is a logical by-product of a belief in the Ptolemaic astronomy combined with a belief in the separable *Psyche* or soul. If we are to look for 'origins' for this part of the Mandaean beliefs, the nearest is the philosophy of Bardaiṣan. According to Bardaiṣan our Lord only raises souls. The body is heavier than the soul and not really akin to it; it cannot cleave to it for ever. Adam's sin prevented souls after death from 'crossing over', while on the other hand the Life or Salvation brought by our Lord was that He enabled souls to cross without hindrance into 'the Bridal-chamber of Light'.[1]

'But why quote from Bardaiṣan?' you will say. Are not the Mandaeans bitterly opposed to Christianity, calling *Eshu Mshiha* a Deceiver and the Holy Spirit a female Demon? Yes, that is true, and yet I believe they are, from the point of view of a scientific classification, properly to be looked upon as Christians, though heretical Christians. They are, in fact, Dissenters, and like other dissenters

[1] See my Essay in C. W. Mitchell, *Ephraim's Prose Refutations*, II, p. cxxv.

from the established forms of religion or philosophy they tend to use a peculiar set of terms, like
those Protestants who would not speak of the
Church but only of the Congregation, and had no
Bishops but only Superintendents.

One preliminary consideration is important. The
Mandaeans may be regarded as heretical Christians: they are certainly not Jews. On this subject
I would refer to the excellent study by the Danish
scholar Dr S. A. Pallis.[1] Dr Pallis does not believe
that there is any direct connexion between Mandaism and Judaism. 'The Mandaeans', he says,
'have made no distinction between Jews and
[Catholic] Christians, or rather when they speak of
Yahutayyē they always think of the Christians and
call them by this name.' He goes on to suggest
that their ideas were confused by the fact that the
Old Testament was a holy book of the Christians.
And, as I have pointed out elsewhere,[2] such knowledge of the Old Testament as the Mandaeans have
does not come from Jewish sources, but from the
Peshitta, the Syriac version of the Bible current in
the Mesopotamian Churches. It was a pity that
Lidzbarski, the learned editor of the Mandaean
sacred books, seems to have been less familiar with
the Syriac Bible than with other branches of
Aramaic literature. All the Hebrew terms, such as
tibil (mentioned above), or *Lewiathan*, or *yama*

[1] S. A. Pallis, *Mandaean Studies*, pp. 115–50 (London,
1926).
[2] *Journ. Theol. Stud.* XXIX, p. 228 f.

d'suf,[1] which might be taken to suggest a direct
acquaintance with the Hebrew Bible or Jewish
tradition, are found similarly transliterated in the
Peshiṭta.[2] This is not what we should find if the
Mandaeans really were descendants of a Jewish
sect, whether heretical or orthodox.

As for the relation of the Mandaeans to Christianity, we ought not to be too much influenced by
the fact that to them *Eshu Mshiha* (Jesus Christ)
is a false prophet, who is also *Nbu*, i.e. Nebo-
Hermes, the planet Mercury, or that his mother is
Ruha d' Kudsha (the Holy Spirit), an evil demon who
is also *Dlibat*, the planet Venus. We are all in this
age of books and diffused education too much influenced by our own personal knowledge of the
beginnings of Christianity, derived from our own
reading of the New Testament itself, and we tend
to think that for those who do not accept orthodox
Church theology there is always the alternative of
a sort of modernist, more or less naturalistic, view
of Jesus Christ who went about doing good. But
for those who are not familiar with the Gospels,
who hear of 'Jesus Christ' or 'Holy Spirit' only as
the sacred deities of a hostile and persecuting
Church, this alternative is not open. And a very
little investigation makes it quite clear that the

---

[1] The (mythical) Red Sea, in which the wicked perish: it
is םי ףס in Hebrew, but is transliterated ܝܡܐ ܕܣܘܦ in
the Peshiṭta, exactly as in Mandaean (see G.L. 55).

[2] Even the *'uphānē* (the 'Wheels') occur in the Peshiṭta
text of Ezek. x 13.

Mandaean hostility to *Eshu Mshiha* is hostility to the fully developed post-Nicene Church. In several places 'Christ' is actually called 'the Byzantine' (*Rumaya*), and further we are told that the disciples of this Christ become 'Christians' (*Kriṣtiani*), and turn into monks and nuns who have no children and who keep fasts and never wear white clothes like the Mandaeans (G.R. II 55). In a word, it is not the Christ of the Gospels, but the Christ of fully developed ecclesiastical organization and policy to which Mandaism is so hostile.[1]

When were Mandaeans persecuted by Christians? It can only have been during the Sasanian Empire, when Christianity was a more or less tolerated religion, whose head—alone recognized as such by the King of Kings—was the Nestorian Catholicus of Seleucia. The Nestorians were reckoned heretical by the Byzantines, but of course their divergences from the Catholic norm were slight in comparison with the Mandaeans, both in organization and doctrine. The Mandaean Religion, as such, was not recognized by the Persian Government: they must have been reckoned as a variety of 'Christians', as in fact they are. '*Amuneil* (i.e. Emmanuel) is his name, *Eshu Mahiana* (i.e. Jesus the Saviour) he calls himself,...when he oppresses you, tell him "We belong to thee". But in your hearts confess him not, and fall not away from the word of your Lord, the high King of Light' (G.R.

---

[1] For this and the following paragraphs, see my above-mentioned study in *Journ. Theol. Stud.* XXIX, pp. 225–37.

I 28). Surely these words from the *Ginza* reflect a time when Mandaeans were willing to let themselves be formally inscribed as Churchmen, though they were not really such.

Words like *Eshu* and *Amuneil* shew that Mandaean transcriptions of Biblical names are often inaccurate. This is no doubt due to ignorance or in some cases (as in *Shum* for Shem, i.e. 'name') to the phonetic laws of the Mandaean language. But occasionally their peculiar religious use of names makes the ordinary use of familiar terms impossible, and other words have to be substituted. *Ruha*, as we have seen, is used by the Mandaeans exclusively for the evil spirit, so they no longer use it, as all other Aramaic dialects do, for 'wind': they use *zika* instead, a word which in Syriac means 'storm'. *Alaha* (i.e. God) has to them the meaning 'false god', so for the true Divine Being they use various substitutes such as 'the Great *Mana*' or *Manda d'Hayyē*. This last term is that from which 'Mandaean' is derived. It means 'the Gnosis of Life' or rather (to use a more familiar term) 'Knowledge of Salvation'. I am not paraphrasing. In Syriac 'life' and 'salvation' with all their derivatives are synonymous in ecclesiastical terminology, and the γνῶσισ σωτηρίασ spoken of in the *Benedictus* (Lk. i 77) is rendered in the Syriac Bible by *madd'ā dhayyē*, which is exactly the same, syllable for syllable, as the Mandaean term.[1] The 'Great *Mana*' means 'the Great Vessel' or 'Garment': I

[1] See Note at end of this chapter.

venture to think it more or less corresponds to the idea of the Valentinian *Pleroma*, something which contained the whole Divinity, in which the Divinity is wrapped, even as the Mandaean is wrapped in his *mana* when he receives the life-giving Baptism.

Well, then, 'Jesus Christ' was to the Mandaean only the Pseudo-Messiah worshipped by the official Christians. Had they a name for the true Jesus? The answer is, Yes; they called Him *Anush* or *Enush*, usually in the form *Anush-uthra*. The word *Uthra* (ܟ̈ܝܬܪܐ), lit. 'wealth', 'treasure', is the Mandaean title for a good spirit, so that *Anush-uthra* might almost be rendered 'Saint Homo'. *Anush* is the same name as the Biblical Patriarch 'Enōsh* (i.e. 'man'), but it is likely that the Mandaean conception of *Anush* as the messenger of the truth is connected with the way in which Jesus in the Gospel calls himself Son of Man (in Syr. *breh d'nāshā*).

What, then, is the career of *Anush-uthra* according to the Mandaeans? In G.R. II 53 and G.R. I 29 we read that Anush-uthra comes into the world in the days of Pilaṭus (or Palṭus, i.e. Pilate) the king of the world; he heals the sick, makes the blind to see, cleanses the lepers, raises the cripples so that they can walk, and makes the deaf and dumb to speak. With the power of the high King of Light he raises the dead. Those who believe in him among the Jews he teaches that there is Life and Death, Light and Darkness and burning Fire, Truth and

Error. Three hundred and sixty Prophets go out of Jerusalem and preach in the name of the Lord of Glory: then Anush-uthra ascends to the Mandaean Paradise and will not be seen again by mankind till the End comes. Before he ascended, however, we read in another place that Anush-uthra will unmask the Deceiver, the Byzantine Christ, who will confess that he is only one of the deceiving Seven Planets: he will be seized by the Jews and crucified (G.R. II 58).

That this tale of the preaching and of the miracles of Anush-uthra in Jerusalem is no isolated patch in the Mandaean construction appears from G.R. XIV 288 f., where true religion is represented as being the doctrine taught by Anush-uthra, and still more from G.R. XV, where Anush-uthra himself sings of his coming into the world. He calls himself the Stranger (*nukraya*, G.R. 328, last line) and says: 'I took a bodily form and appeared in Jerusalem. I spoke with my voice and preached, and became a Healer for Miriai: a Healer for Miriai I became, and healed her from head to foot. I was called Healer of the Truth (*kushta*), who heals and takes no fee' (G.R. 331 f.).[1] This is followed among other things by the mission of 365 disciples. Clearly we have here a parallel to what we read in G.R. I and II; it is the same doctrine that is set forth.

[1] The emphasis on the healing of Miriai, the faithful convert and disciple (see Lk. viii 2), is enough to shew that this Mandaean figure has been developed out of Mary Magdalene, not out of Mary the mother of Jesus as Lidzbarski (*Johannesbuch*, p. 125) imagines.

The Mandaeans, then, rejected the Christ of the Catholic Church, born of a woman and crucified, but they accepted the Stranger who appeared in Jerusalem in the days of Pilate, who healed the sick and taught the true and life-giving doctrine, and who ascended in due course when his work was done to his own place in the world of Light. This Personage is called the Stranger, but he is no stranger to the modern student of Christian antiquity: it is clearly the Manichaean Jesus, a personage adopted by Mani from Jesus of Marcion.[1] In other words it is no new controversial figment of the Mandaeans.

The Marcionites in the fifth and sixth centuries were an unlicensed and vanishing society. But they had once been a great factor in the Christianity of the Euphrates Valley, as is clear from the polemics of Ephraim and still more from the influence which they had on the new theology of Mani. I am not suggesting that the Mandaeans are Marcionites in disguise: what I do suggest is that Theodore bar Konai was right when he tells us that Mandaean doctrine is partly derived from the Marcionites, and I think we can say with confidence that that part is their 'Christology', that Anush-uthra is the Marcionite Jesus.

From Manichaeism the Mandaeans derived their

---

[1] Several passages in Ephraim's *Prose Refutations of Marcion* seem to indicate a Marcionite doctrine of two Messiahs, the false and the true: see Mitchell, II, p. xxxviii, l. 14; p. xlviii, l. 18; p. xlix, l. 24.

conception of the High King of Light and His glorious and peaceful realm far beyond the heaven and earth of this evil world. His Five good attributes, His seat in the North, and other details, seem to have come direct from Mani's presentation of the 'King of the Paradises of Light'. Further, the Mandaean formula of Confession in G.R. II 61 ff. (especially 63, end)[1] recalls the Manichaean *Khuastuanift*. But the connexion of Mandaism with Manichaeism does not seem to me so intimate as its connexion with the religion of Marcion.

In one point, of course, Mandaism differs from the organization of the Marcionites and the Manichees, in that marriage is not only permitted but commanded. Mandaism further differs from most forms of Christian practice, in that Baptism is not administered once and for all, but is often repeated, as often as required. According to Epiphanius the Marcionites permitted a second and third baptism. The Mandaean repeated baptisms might be reconciled to Marcionite theory as an extension of their custom. It is noteworthy that particular lustrations are commanded to Mandaeans in connexion both with marriage and cohabitation (G.R. 1 14, and elsewhere).[2]

Of course it would be hopelessly perverse to attempt to derive all Mandaean mythology and praxis from Mesopotamian Marcionite Christianity alone. I am not here primarily concerned

[1] *Lidzbarski*, p. 57: cf. my *Religion of the Manichees*, p. 57 f.
[2] *Lidzbarski*, pp. 16, 35.

with Mandaism in itself, but with the use that has been made during the last fifteen years of Mandaean parallels to New Testament ideas and phrases, the use, I mean, whereby these phrases have been treated as independent parallels, not as borrowings, often unintelligent borrowings or adaptations, from the Syriac Bible. So far as I know, the only protests that have been raised have been those of Dr Pallis in Copenhagen, Prof. Peterson in Bonn, Père Lagrange in the *Revue Biblique*, besides my article in the *Journal of Theological Studies*. Lately, however, our protests have been reinforced by a study of the Mandaean Baptismal Liturgy by Prof. H. Lietzmann of Berlin in the *Sitzungsberichte* of the Prussian Academy for 1930 (*Phil.-Hist. Kl.* XXVII, pp. 596–608). Prof. Lietzmann goes through the notices of John the Baptist in the Mandaean writings, and shews that they belong to the later stages of their tradition, that they have no other basis than the Canonical Gospels, and that there is nothing to connect the Mandaeans with conjectural followers of John. Further, he compares the Mandaean Baptismal rite with the Nestorian Order of Baptism, and comes to the conclusion that the Mandaean rite is actually derived from the Nestorian, even to the use of the word 'Jordan' in the sense of baptismal water![1] Anyone who has read a good modern description of the Mandaeans and their way of life—I can recommend Mrs Drower's, to be found in the

[1] *Lietzmann*, p. 602.

114

Quest, XVI (1924-5), pp. 80-92, 217-25—will understand that Mandaean Baptisms are the centre of the Mandaean Religion, far more than the fairytales that they have inherited or invented about Angels and Demons.

'But after all', some one may say, 'you began with the Left-hand *Ginza*, with the *Massektas* that speed the soul to the heavenly regions after it has left the body for ever. You said that the belief about the fate of the soul was the true essence of Mandaism. Surely that is Gnostic?' Yes, central also to Mandaean Religion is the doctrine of the ascent of the enlightened soul after its separation from the body through the 'custodies' (*mattartas*), i.e. guarded frontiers, through which only those provided with the seal acquired in Mandaean baptism can pass. And further there is the peculiar Mandaean mythology—Abatur, Ptahil, Ur, a series of Demiurgic beings unlike in name and function from anything known elsewhere. These may be of Mesopotamian origin: no one has yet suggested a really satisfactory derivation for 'Abatur' or 'Ptahil', who occupy somewhat the same place in the Mandaean system (or rather systems) as Jaldabaoth does in some Western Gnostic systems. It may be noted that 'Crun, the great mountain of flesh', that tries to swallow Hibil-Ziwa (G.R. 143), seems to be a far-off reminiscence of Κρόνοσ, of Saturn, not the planet but the banished father who used to swallow his children and now sits in Tartarus. If this be so,

115   8-2

there is also a Greek, i.e. Western, element in Mandaean mythology.

I should like here to put forward the conjecture that Ur, the Lord of Darkness, the worst of demons, who swallows souls, is a deformation of ὕλη. *Hyle*, ܗܘܠܐ, is the evil element in Marcion's system:[1] this explanation of the name fits excellently with the part that *Ur*, עור, plays in Mandaean mythology. As for the form, Mandaean ע corresponds to Syriac *ḥu* in the word עוצא, 'leaf':[2] Mandaean ר corresponds to Syriac *l* in the word תארמידא, 'disciple' (Syriac *talmīdā*); and an unaccented final vowel can easily fall out, as in עטאך *eṭak*, which comes from the Greek τάχα.[3] Thus every apparent irregularity has its appropriate etymological parallel.[4]

But as for what may be called more particularly the 'Gnostic' part of the Mandaean theology, the doctrine that the human soul is imprisoned in an alien, non-redeemable body, from which it escapes at death but even then cannot win its way to its true home outside the spheres which encompass this world, save only if it have assimilated the true

[1] See Mitchell's *Ephraim*, 1 70 f., 140 ff.

[2] Nöldeke, *Mandäische Grammatik*, p. 61.

[3] *Ibid.* p. 202.

[4] I should like also here to suggest that *Ḳolasta* (קולאסתא), the name of the Mandaean Hymn-book, is not derived from the Arabic خلاصة (i.e. 'quintessence'), but is simply the feminine of the Syriac word *ḳullāsā* (ܩܘܠܣܐ), meaning 'praise' or 'laud'. This word is ultimately derived from καλῶς, and is quite common in Syriac literature.

knowledge during this life, this also can be traced
in the Euphrates Valley in ancient Christian circles,
for it is the doctrine of Bardaiṣan. Bardaiṣan was
a philosopher, a man of culture and science, as
such things were understood in his days, with some
astronomical knowledge of his own. So far as his
ideas have been transmitted to us, he does not
speak of monstrous genii with fantastic forms and
names, but of Fate and Free-will, of the Planets, of
the Heavenly Powers on the right or the left:
what may be called the fairy-tale element is absent.
But his mythology does speak of souls hindered at
the crossing,[1] and kept in seven Limbos (*mā‘ōnē*),[2]
which correspond in function at least to the
Mandaean celestial Prisons (*maṭṭartas*). Moreover
madd‘a, the Syriac word from which *manda* is actually derived, was the name Bardaiṣan used for the
Divine Reason or Gnosis that dwells in man.[3]

As I said at the beginning, I venture to think
that modern writers about 'the Gnosis' have not
always considered that some of the resemblances
between some of the very different 'Gnostic'
systems may come from a common understanding
of the actual facts which ultimately gave rise to the
pseudo-science of Astrology, facts that had to be
taken account of when once they had been apprehended. The Ptolemaic system, though now antiquated, was in its day up-to-date science, based on

[1] *Mitchell*, II, p. lxxvii: see also p. cxxx.
[2] *Ibid*. pp. lxxvii and xcvii.
[3] *Ibid*. p. lxxiii.

actual observation of facts. When Milton's 'meek-eyed Peace...came softly sliding Down through the turning sphere' from Heaven, it was really through a series of spheres that she had to pass. The discovery of the regular but independent motion of the Planets was accounted for by the doctrine that they were fixed each in its own sphere, which apparently no other star could penetrate. Heaven therefore was not open as it seemed: it was surrounded by crystal spheres, transparent indeed but impenetrable. Granted that the Soul when released from the Body flew up towards Heaven, how could it get through the spheres on its way home?

My point is that this difficulty presents itself naturally, is a natural question to be asked. It is not wonderful that several systems have a doctrine of 'wards' to be passed, in number corresponding generally with the number of the Planets. Sometimes the stress was laid on past good conduct, sometimes on the possession of secret knowledge: what seemed evident was that some passport was necessary before the soul could read its title clear to mansions in the skies—or rather, beyond the skies. Wherever therefore the doctrine of the 'spheres' was accepted we find doctrines of how to get past them, corresponding in part to old tales of how to pass the fabled rivers of Hades.

In any case, what we know of Bardaiṣan's cosmogony is enough to shew analogies with the substructure underlying the fantastic and complicated Mandaean fairy-tales. The important thing is, that Bardaiṣan belongs to the region of the Euphrates Valley. We need not go to the sects described by Irenaeus and Hippolytus and Epiphanius for analogies to Mandaism. The Mandaeans live in Babylonia. Their sacred writings were compiled some seventy years after the coming of Islam, i.e. not before A.D. 700. Their founder, that is to say the founder of Mandaism in its present form, according to the only tradition we have, was a wandering ascetic from Adiabene, whose doctrines were partly borrowed from those of the Marcionites and the Manichees, both known to have been influential in Mesopotamia generally. It requires very strong detailed evidence to make it probable that any parts of the system which do not seem to come from Marcionites or Manichees were derived directly from a Mediterranean source. The Biblical knowledge of the Mandaeans can all be traced to a study of the Peshiṭta, the Bible of the official Christians of Babylonia, including their unsympathetic portrait of Jesus Christ. The Mandaean Anush-uthra, on the other hand, is not a mere pale reflexion of the Church's Jesus Christ, but the Marcionite (and Manichaean) Jesus: all that is said of Anush-uthra, including the figure of Miriai, a queer reminiscence of Mary Magdalene, is ultimately derived from the Lucan Gospel as curtailed and arranged by Marcion.

In Bardaiṣan we have an educated Gnostic's doctrine of a modified astrological Fate, including the soul's fate after death. In Mandaism we have a somewhat similar doctrine, as seen through the medium of oral lore and a tradition preserved by wandering mendicants. Even though a feature here and there may be recognized as the lineal descendant of ancient speculations of the age of Valentinus, we cannot expect it to be more faithfully preserved than the features of the Marcionite Jesus are preserved in the Mandaean Anush-uthra. In other words, Mandaism may be interesting in itself, but it is useless to go to it as a key to unlock the mysteries of early Christian development.

NOTE

ON THE PHRASE *MANDA D'HAYYE*

As I said on p. 109 the Mandaean term *Manda d'Hayyē* actually occurs in the Syriac text of the *Benedictus* (Lk. i 77). This is duly acknowledged by Lidzbarski (*Johannesbuch*, p. xvii, note 2), but Lagarde's remark there quoted is misleading. Lagarde says 'Lucas i 77 γνῶσισ σωτηρίασ ܡܕܥܐ ܕܚܝܐ übersetzt, während sonst σωτηρία ܦܘܪܩܢܐ ist'. This remark was made in 1890, before the discovery of the Sinai Palimpsest had enlarged our knowledge of early Syriac ecclesiastical diction.

First, as to σωτηρία and σώζειν. The 'Old Syriac' Version regularly represented these words by 'life' (ܚܝܐ) and 'cause to live' (ܐܚܝ), even in such passages as Matt. viii 25, where the cry of the disciples in the boat—Κύριε, σῶσον —is rendered in *S* (*hiat C*) 'Our Lord, make us live!' In the Peshiṭta, a revision of the 'Old Syriac' made about A.D. 412, this curious rendering is generally retained, but a more literal one is now and then substituted. For instance, in Matt. viii 25 the Peshiṭta has 'Our Lord, deliver us' (ܦܪܘܩܢ). As for the noun σωτηρία, the rendering 'life' is allowed to remain in Lk. i 77, xix 9, and Joh. iv 22, but ܦܘܪܩܢܐ, 'deliverance', is substituted in Lk. i 69 (a word reserved by the 'Old Syriac' for λύτρωσις); and the resumptive σωτηρίαν of Lk. i 71, for which *S* has 'and He hath snatched us away to life', becomes 'that He might deliver us' in the Peshiṭta. Notwithstanding these corrections, 'life'—though in Syriac, as in Hebrew and also Mandaean, it is a masculine plural—continued to be the conventional equivalent for 'salvation', as may be seen from Jude 3, where in the post-Peshiṭta version 'our common salvation' is rendered 'the life of us in common' (ܚܝܐ ܕܠܢ ܓܘܢܐ).

The word ܡܕܥܐ (i.e. *madde͑ā*, with hard *d*, like ܡܢܕܥܐ) is a perfectly regular formation from ܝܕܥ, 'to know'. It occurs also in Jewish Aramaic, in some dialects of which the -*dd*- in the middle is turned into -*nd*-, just as in Mandaean. In Syriac the word is used not so much for 'knowledge' as for 'intelligence' or 'reason'. Bardaiṣan calls *madd͑ā* the strange and divine leaven in the soul, the soul being in itself without knowledge (*ʾīda͑thā*): in other words, it is Reason regarded as a superadded faculty in the human make-up. It is therefore exactly that supernatural understanding of divine things which is meant by *gnosis* as a technical term. The *Manda d'Hayyē* is exactly the personified Gnosis.

'Far be it for me', says Miriai the true Mandaean, 'to love him whom I have hated; far be it for me to hate whom I have loved;

Nay, far be it for me my Lord Manda d'Hayyē to hate, who is for me a support in the world,

A support is He to me in the world, and a Helper in the place of Light.'

As this extract shews,[1] *Manda d'Hayyē* is fully personified, a Being capable of inspiring romantic affection. Miriai is the Mandaean name for Mary, i.e. Mary Magdalene (Lk. viii 2), the disciple of Jesus. No doubt the ultimate historical fact, according to our Western ideas of concrete fact, upon which

---

[1] *Johannesbuch* 131, p. 129; *Ḳolasta* XLIV, p. 211 f.

the poetical lines I have just quoted is based, is the affection and gratitude which Jesus inspired in Mary Magdalene. But the Mandaean Religion is altogether alien to concrete history. As with the Manichees, they confuse the Prophet, his symbol, his doctrine: in fact they distrust the concrete human personality, as does the 'Gnostic' author of the *Acts of John*.[1] 'Miriai' has no doubt come into the Mandaean mythology through the Marcionite Gospel with its de-humanized Jesus: *Anush-uthra*—'Saint Homo', as we might call Him—is not really more human than *Manda d'Hayyē*, the doctrine proclaimed by Saint Homo, but is also not less human. So in the end the words of Miriai do re-echo some of the loyalty and devotion of the orthodox Christian for his Lord and Saviour.

In any case, to translate *Manda d'Hayyē* by γνῶσισ ζωῆσ, and not γνῶσισ σωτηρίασ, is to beg the question of the origin of the term.

[1] See M. R. James, *Apocryphal N.T.*, p. 256.

Chapter V

THE CHURCH AND THE
OLD TESTAMENT

WE have glanced at Gnostic theology in its philosophic bloom and its mythological decay. What had the Church to offer as an alternative? Harnack says somewhere that in the great struggle of the Diocletian persecution, at the beginning of the fourth century, the two sides, Christianity and Paganism, had only one theology but two rival mythologies. Whether the epigram be Harnack's or another's, and whether it expresses the state of things accurately, does not matter: it is near enough to historical truth to be a good starting-point.

What is meant by the one theology is the victory of Monotheism, tempered by subordinate hero-cults. On the Pagan side many of the old cults of Gods and Goddesses, Heroes and Saviours, were alive and flourishing, but the unity of the supreme Divine Power was generally recognized in theory. From the time of Elagabalus, culminating in Aurelian, the supremacy of the Unconquerable Sun, unique and all-vivifying, had come into prominence. The Zeus of official worship was in practice a name of the Unconquerable Sun, as well as of the Open Sky, always present and always the same everywhere. Similarly the Christians were consciously monotheistic; but they refused to identify their GOD with 'Zeus'. On the other hand, for those who wanted a less august worship side by side with that of the Supreme Deity, there had grown up among Christians the cult of the Martyrs, beginning with the local Martyrs of whom the several Churches were proud; and these local cults were becoming more and more universal in the case of the greater and more notable Saints.

I am not wishing to press the analogy or to maintain a paradox. No doubt, when examined carefully, the Christians and their opponents had different theologies, but there were also great resemblances. There was superstition among the Christians on the one hand; and, on the other, the theology of the higher Paganism had become so enlightened that it is an open question whether the theological ideas of the Hermetic writings are, or are not, independent of Christian ideas. This literature, we may remember, is quoted by Lactantius, writing just after the Diocletian persecution came to an end, so that, whatever the origin of the Hermetic writings may have been, they must then have represented a living movement of non-Christian contemporary thought.

There was also assimilation in Christian thought about the state of the dead. The baptismal profession of Christian faith still expressed belief in the resurrection of the flesh, as indeed it does to this day, but the emotional value of this inherited dogma was already overshadowed by a vivid belief in the intermediate state, the state of the dead, good and bad, immediately after death. The Martyrs at least, so all Christians believed, had gone to reign with Christ—or rather their souls and spirits had gone there, for their venerated bones were the special treasure of the Christians still on earth. At any rate they were already in conscious bliss.

The old Christian belief that GOD had appointed a day in which He would judge the world by the man whom He had ordained, in which all men of all ages would rise again in their bodies and receive their due punishment or reward, still survived, but what had that stupendous Assize come to mean? The dead were already judged, were already receiving their reward. In terms of literature, the doctrine of the Apocalypse of Peter, however uncanonical, had superseded that of the Apocalypse of John. The assurance of 'immortality' was no doubt stronger among the Christians than the Pagans, and the means of obtaining a happy lot after death were different, but the state was much the same. The blessed souls domiciled in the Milky Way of whom we read in the *Somnium Scipionis*, the initiated Gnostic after death who flies unimpeded through the spheres, the glorified Martyrs of the Catholic Church, these are all in much the same state of existence: they are in heaven, but they have not been resurrected. Here again there has been assimilation of ideas, away from the early Jewish and Christian presentation towards the ideas of Greek speculation.

Yet one thing is certain. We modern historians of thought may see the resemblances between Pagan and Christian Religion at the time of their last great open struggle for ascendancy: at the time, what the Pagans and Christians were acutely conscious of was their incompatible difference. In what did this consist? The epigram I quoted at the beginning placed the difference in their mythology. What is implied by this?

If we reply that the Christians believed in the Bible, while the Pagans had nothing but their false and fantastic legends of the Gods, we are giving the old-fashioned answer. This answer I believe to be essentially true, but at the present day it requires a good deal of reformulation. I propose to consider at some length what belief in the Bible really implies, and in what way it is essentially different from the Pagan account of the origin of Gods and men.

We cannot now, without definition, contrast 'Bible truth' with 'heathen fables'. And it is exactly in those parts, upon the historical accuracy of which old-time believers laid most stress, that the literal truth of the Bible is now most called in question. The creation of the world in six days, Adam and Eve, Noah's Flood (in the sense of a world-wide Deluge),—these things have dropped out of our geological manuals and our primers of Ancient History. I am not one of those who think this is a matter of no consequence for the present and the future of the Christian Faith. The need for a reconstruction and revision of our theological theories about the origin of things, including Man, is coming more and more to be felt among thoughtful Christians, though useful reconstruction does not make much progress.

Nevertheless the Old Testament is in the main a book of history, of history rather than of systematic theology. Even the legislation, though regarded as Divine, is couched in historical form. The contrast, then, between the religion of the Christians and that of the Pagans in Diocletian's day, if we neglect the mere legends of the Gods and bear in mind such expositions of Paganism as that of Sallustius, is the contrast between an historical account and a philosophical account. Or rather, since 'historical' is often used in modern times in the sense of 'truly historical', let us say between an annalistic and a systematic account.

Annalistic or systematic—let us consider a few leading Christian documents which are systematic, that we may better appreciate how the Bible differs from them. I am thinking of such documents as the Creeds, the Church Catechism, the *Summa* of Thomas Aquinas. These are all very valuable documents, excellent in their way and in their place. But the Bible—and here I am thinking particularly of the Old Testament—is different. It is a set of writings which, taken together, give an account of how the Religion of the Jews came to be what it was about the Christian era. A cursory study of this literature brings out the fact that the outstanding achievement of the Israelite race consists in new ideas about the relation of moral conduct to true religion. These ideas are to be found in the utterances of the Prophets, a great chain of seers of whom the greatest names are Amos, Hosea, Isaiah, Jeremiah, the Second Isaiah, and Ezekiel.

It is most important to include Ezekiel, if we wish to understand the essential difference between Jewish and Greek Religion and justify to ourselves the 'narrowness' and 'exclusiveness' of Judaism and of its daughter, Christianity. Even the causes of this narrowness are historical rather than systematic, they are the result of a special development, the history of which is to be found woven into the structure of the Bible. We can now give a more or less reasoned account of this development, helped thereto not only by methodical study of the Bible and by setting the various parts of it in their true chronology and environment, but also by the possession of an evolutionary philosophy, a philosophy which sees living truth in growth and change and 'epigenesis', rather than in a static perfection.

But this evolutionary philosophy is essentially a product of our own times. The times were not ripe for it in the age of Diocletian, or indeed in any age until the present day. Therefore the only form in which such a philosophy could be held in ancient times was an annalistic form, something which had as its Palladium an account of a development rather than an infallible exposition of the final stage.

Let us think for a moment what we have come to believe that the Old Testament really is, and then at the reasons which led the Church, in its formative stage, to cling to it in preference to any system of Gnostic construction. This, I may remark in passing, was the real alternative. The Creeds of the fourth and fifth centuries were attempts at short and yet authoritative statements of Christian Doctrine, but by that time the main lines of Christian Doctrine had already crystallized and, moreover, the Creeds all profess to be founded on the statements of Holy Scripture. With what difficulty was the term *homoousion* inserted in the Creed, just because it is not actually found in the Bible! The real battle in the second century centred round the position of the Old Testament.

What, then, is the Old Testament? It is the collection of the sacred Books of the Jews, and were it not so familiar to us from childhood we should recognize more easily that it is a very extraordinary collection. What can we learn from it? We learn from it the process by which the Jewish Religion came to be what it was, an unique phenomenon in the then new post-Alexandrian civilization, indeed an unique phenomenon in the ancient world generally. The Old Testament may be described as the record of two controversies, both of great importance and interest in themselves, and still more so by reason of the solution they received in fully developed Judaism. They may be called, for short, 'Nature-Religion or Social Religion' and 'Priest or Prophet'.

Let me indicate, in the fewest possible words, what I mean. Man's life depends upon the food-supply, and this, both for man and beast, depends upon the weather. How can we secure good harvests? One ancient answer, as we all know, is that if we cut the crops with the right ceremonies, and give the local Unseen Powers the right kind of tribute, they may be favourable to us and give us a good harvest next season. This is what is called in the Old Testament 'Baal-worship'. It is a sort of magic, a sort of unscientific science, what I called just now Nature-Religion. Beside this, and for the most part in opposition to it, there is in the Old Testament another Religion. Man by himself is weak, but he has a power of combination with his fellows that makes him master of all living things, and if he be oppressed by other men it is by combination with friends that he can free himself. But combination involves give and take, in a word, morality, discipline, forbearance. Nowhere, let me point out, is this clearer than in War. If the members of a clan be fighting together side by side for a common object they must be ready to give up individual advantages for the common good, they must obey their leader, they must work and fight and if necessary die for the common cause. And in primitive society all this is under the sanction of Religion. The God of the clan fights for His own clansmen and gives them, if He be stronger than the God of their enemies, victory in battle.

It was in war that religious patriotism was most clearly displayed, but it shewed itself also in peace. The tradition says that Moses brought out the Israelites from Egypt, but it also makes him the legislator who formulated the rules that ought to obtain between one Israelite and another. And both parts of Moses' work were accomplished with the help and the sanction of the GOD whom he taught his countrymen to call by a new Name. To Hebrew thought the Name implied the character, and the new Name, however pronounced, whether Yahweh or Yahoh, implied patriotism and civil justice.

Here then we have two distinct conceptions of Religion: in the one it means the practices and the customs that were believed to ensure the due abundance of the kindly fruits of the earth, in the other it means patriotism and civil justice. In the Old Testament the former conception is associated with the Baalim, the local Genius of each district and with the immemorial rites locally practised; the Lord GOD whom Moses made known to Israel is associated with the other conception, with everything that makes for true patriotism or true civil justice. I stress the adjective, for we see in the words of the Prophets an expansion and a deepening of what true patriotism might mean.

The other great controversy with which the Old Testament is concerned is that between 'Priest' and

'Prophet'. I need not go into details, for most of it is familiar ground. The Priest is the religious professional: the essential thing is that religion is his profession, his trade. The main method of communicating with the Gods in ancient times was by sacrifices, so that conducting sacrifices was one of the main duties of priests; but besides this it was the regular duty of the priest to declare the will of the GOD, whether by Oracles, or casting the sacred Lot, or by his knowledge of the ancient customs. He was usually attached to a particular shrine, and the central government, if at all powerful, can generally exercise a good deal of control over a local sanctuary. All these considerations tend to make the Priest a bulwark of conservatism, not the conservatism that looks back to 'the good old times' as compared with present abuses, but the conservatism of the existing system.

The Prophet was quite different, and the greater Prophets of Israel represent a quite peculiar development. The essence of the Prophet is that it is understood that GOD Himself was speaking by him. To get a just idea of this claim we must begin on a much lower level than what would be implied nowadays by these words. We need not go outside the Bible. We see from the old tales in 1 Samuel that when Saul was 'among the Prophets' it meant that he had been seized with a fit of wild religious frenzy, such as we are told comes over a Negro at an emotional Camp-meeting.[1] We say in such cases

[1] 1 Sam. xix 24.

that the man has lost his self-control; the Orientals say he is 'possessed': that is, an unseen but real spirit, good or evil, has come and taken possession of his intelligence, so that the words he may utter are not the man's own but those of the alien spirit.

Such was the Prophet in Israel when we first come across him. But there followed a strange transformation, the most remarkable and important fact in Israelite history. The essence of the Prophet is his enthusiasm. He speaks with authority, because he believes, and those who hear him believe, that what he says is not his own but the Oracle of the GOD. Nothing less than this can nerve a man, and particularly an Oriental, to run counter to the King, the Government, to those who have official position in the State and in Religion, above all to the all-pervading authority of Custom. A consciousness of direct inspiration from GOD makes a man free of all other authority: to be under compulsion from GOD is to be free of every other sort of dominion.

So the Prophet, like the Mohammedan Dervish, was free to do and say what his inner impulse moved him to do or say. 'A *consciousness* of direct inspiration'—the prophet-dervishes whom Saul joined were not properly conscious at all, they were drunk with their enthusiasm. The strange transformation of which I spoke was the rise of a chain of Seers who had the prophetic enthusiasm but remained sober and conscious of their mission. Elijah, Amos, Jeremiah, Ezekiel,—these four are the most important links: they represent the transformation of the religion of the Israelites out of something almost indistinguishable from ordinary Semitic heathenism into the peculiar Jewish system, which is presupposed in the writings of the New Testament and which still survives in its two children, Christianity and the Rabbinical Religion.

Each of the four—Elijah, Amos, Jeremiah, Ezekiel—had a peculiar relation of antagonism or alliance with the Priests of their day, and equally a peculiar relation with regard to that other controversy, which I have called 'Nature-Religion or Social Religion'. It would take too long to summarize the familiar tale of the message of Amos and Jeremiah, though they do represent a revolution in religious thought. They were in antagonism to the Priests of their day, and to the time-hallowed Nature-Religion with which the Priests were identified. The moral denunciations of Amos sound to-day like religious commonplace; in Amos's day they were revolutionary paradox. Jeremiah may almost be said to have found out personal religion, independent of national worship. Though he lived to see all the externals of worship swept away, he still had communion with his GOD. Before him Religion had been always more or less national, civic, communal.

But the lofty peak reached by Jeremiah was by no means the last stage in the development of Old Testament Religion. In the end the great controversies of which I have spoken had a most unforeseen issue, unforeseen that is by Amos and Jeremiah, though it embodied the essential victory of their ideas. They had been in opposition to the established worship and to the priests, not because the worship was ritualistic or the priests a professional class, but because the ritualistic worship had no concern with social abuses and was in some ways itself immoral, and because the priests were the champions of this worship and were not the champions of social morality.

Herein lies the importance of Ezekiel. In him we see the coalescence of the prophetic and priestly ideals. He was a Priest, one of the first batch of exiles, and his prophetic Visions came to him in Babylonia, far from the Holy Land of Palestine. He was as keen about moral conduct as Amos himself, and he received the news of the fall of Jerusalem as calmly as Amos contemplated the fall of Samaria. But he believed that in GOD'S good time the nation would be restored, and then the very centre of the restored community was to be a reformed Temple served by worthy priests.

Fifty years after Ezekiel had published his sketch of a restored Israel his dream materialized, for in 521 B.C., exactly a century after Josiah's Reform, and two centuries after the fall of Samaria, the faithful Jews restarted the worship of the LORD on the site of the old Temple in Jerusalem. It was a day of small things, for the community was poor, but it was the triumph of that peculiar blend of prophetic and priestly ideals of which Ezekiel is the mouthpiece. This henceforth was the Jewish Religion, the religion which is the background of the New Testament.

Which had won, Prophet or Priest, Nature-Religion or Social Religion? The Priests were in possession: the race of Jewish Prophets, true and false, died out, but mainly because their cause had triumphed. In post-exilic Judaism there was, so to speak, a Constitution. The ancient customs of Israel had been during the Exile finally codified and woven together with two or three ancient collections of the national traditions of the heroic period. These customs included both the rudiments of a civil code and the regulations of sacrificial worship. The result is what we call the Pentateuch. As a literary work it is perhaps cumbrous and ill-proportioned, but so are many binding legal documents. The important thing is that it was binding on all the Jews, both priests and people. The Priest became a constitutional priest, and the layman could and did know as much about a priest's duties and privileges as the priest himself. Duty, both ritual and moral, was henceforth a matter of public knowledge, and it was all a part of Religion.

Moreover that Religion was in the main Social Religion, while Nature-Religion received a sufficient measure of recognition. In the main, fully-developed post-exilic Judaism is a Rule of life and of conduct. Even the weekly Sabbath-taboo is grounded in one form of its prescription on a humanitarian basis. And the immorality formerly connected with the Nature-Feasts, against which the Prophets so often protest, quite disappeared, though the connexion of Passover with first-fruits and of Pentecost with wheat-harvest is still perceptible. The connexion of Tabernacles with the joyous time of vintage is too obvious ever to have been in doubt, but even there an effort was made to connect it in thought with the legendary conditions of the days of Moses.

This is the Jewish Religion, the Religion set forth in its growth and its completion in the Old Testament. In some ways it does not strike us as so peculiar as it ought to strike us, but in very truth it was a new thing, unique in the Graeco-Roman world. The Greeks, and after them the Romans, were very much concerned with Duty, but to them Duty had little to do with Religion; it was a branch of Philosophy. It was the special characteristic of the Jewish Religion that Duty and Ritual, social conduct and public worship, were all parts of it, and it was the duty of the layman as much as that of the priest to know and meditate upon all parts of it alike. As a result the Jew was ready to die for his Religion, while the immemorial religious customs of Greek and Roman sank to the level of public spectacles. Religion to the Jew was a living force, because it was his concern, not merely the concern of a professional class.

The above is not exactly the account of the Old Testament given by Irenaeus in the *Epideixis*!

Irenaeus uses the Old Testament after the manner of his day: his own view of the world and of the place of man in it was in many respects much nearer to that of the Gnostics whose speculations we have been considering than it is to ours. The parts of Bible history upon which Irenaeus chiefly laid stress, as did also our grandfathers, are those tales in Genesis which we have learnt to look upon as folklore. But it is not the system of Irenaeus which directly concerns us now. The important thing is that his theology, in opposition to the Gnostics and also to Marcion, accepts the Old Testament *en bloc*, not merely those parts of it which can easily be used as a proof or illustration of a second-century theological system, whether that of Irenaeus or of some other. That was the only way in which the Old Testament could be preserved through the Dark Ages, as may be seen by the fate of the rejected Book of Enoch.

We come back to the point from which we started. The Church accepted the Old Testament as its authoritative mythology, and that prevented it from ever becoming quite identical with the pagan Religion which it supplanted, monotheistic and sacramental as that Religion tended to be. And, as I said above, this Christian mythology was annalistic. Like the pagan Religion there was an account of the beginnings of things, and in the beginning things were alleged to have happened which had a decisive influence over all human life and destiny. So it was with Osiris, with Attis, with the Titans, with Hermes Trismegistos. But then there was a gap. How different is the Christian Sacred Drama, enacted not at the beginning but at the end of the ages, and yet linked up with the beginning by the whole religious history of a chosen Nation! A long history—that was the only form in which anything approximately equivalent to an organic evolutionary process could be apprehended in ancient times.

It is a remarkable fact that the New Testament is as annalistic, occasional, unsystematic, as the Old. How different it is in form and general construction from the Kor'an or the Mandaean Ginza, or (so far as we can reconstruct them) the Manichaean Scriptures! The Letters of Paul are occasional writings: even if we regard Romans i–xiv and Ephesians as theological treatises in the form of letters, yet even Romans was used by its author as a letter, as we see from Romans xv, which he must have added as a sort of covering letter or postscript. The Four Gospels are a miscellaneous group, two of which are directly based on a third. The greater part of Acts, though of very great historical interest, is very unlike a Sacred Book. What should we think of, say, one of the 'Sacred Books of the Eàst', six per cent. of which proved on examination to consist of the detailed story of a shipwreck? The remarkable thing is not that Luke should have recorded the shipwreck, where indeed he and his friend S. Paul were actually present, though playing a very passive rôle, but that his record should have become Holy Scripture without drastic curtailment. Can we imagine Acts xxvii becoming part of the *Corpus Valentinianum*? Of course, if such a piece of literature was already part of the sacred writings cherished by a religious body, from which he was a Dissenter, he might have retained it and allegorized it, but he would hardly have adopted it on his own initiative.

And there is yet another thing about which the tale of S. Paul's sea-voyage and shipwreck may put us on our guard. The writer was one of the Four Evangelists, one of those who drew up, from whatever authorities or traditions, the only accounts of Jesus Christ we possess. I am quite willing to acknowledge that the account of the shipwreck has been a little 'written up'. The speech of S. Paul in Acts xxvii 21–6 is rather different from the words which a phonograph might have caught coming through the howling of the wind. But it is the work of one who is really interested in incidents and historical situations, not dominated by dogmatic considerations and Scriptural reminiscences. Both Mark and Luke appear to me to be historical in intention: they wish to tell their readers a tale which they believe to be true.

The interests of the Evangelists whom we call Matthew and John seem to me to be less historical and more directly didactic; no doubt when they made changes they were all in the direction of the theological ideas which they had at heart, in

Matthew the fulfilment of Old Testament prophecy, in John the peculiar Logos-theology. But Matthew's dependence on his main authority, viz. the Gospel of Mark itself, is so marked that 'Matthew' remains an historical document: if Mark were not extant, we should be able to extract most of his historical information from the latter half of the Gospel of Matthew. 'John' is far less annalistic, far less naïve, but even in the case of the Fourth Gospel the epoch-making fact of Mark's narrative, working on the Church partly by its direct influence, but still more being incorporated into and forming the background of Matthew and Luke, caused the new Ephesian estimate of the essential teaching of the Incarnate Son of God to be set in a narrative framework. The four accounts of Jesus, which the Church came to cherish as authoritative, are all annalistic: all four, in their several ways, do set forth a 'Christ after the flesh'. How sparing are the Gospels (and Acts) in giving us teaching from the risen Jesus, how full on the contrary are the accounts given of it in Gnostic documents! The Gnostics did not like the annalistic; they wanted the systematic, something not conditioned by time and environment.

I spoke just now of the 'epoch-making fact of Mark's narrative'. I know quite well that this is a contentious phrase, so that a few words justifying it may not be out of place here. I do not need to go over the familiar ground of Synoptic criticism: what I wish to explain is the view I take of the place of the Gospel tales in Christendom before Mark's Gospel was published, i.e. about 65 or 66 A.D.

Frankly, I think very few Christians had been instructed in them, or even had heard them told. What the Germans call *Gemeinde-Theologie*, the popular consensus, produced the Creed (or something like it) and did not produce the narrative of Mark. Luke's patron, 'the Rt. Hon. Theophilus', had been instructed in the Christian Religion, but there is nothing to suggest that this included any more of the Gospel history than is included in something like the Apostles' Creed. What Theophilus had been taught was not (as I venture to think) tales about Jesus; it was more likely to have been those first principles of which the author of the Epistle to the Hebrews speaks—repentance, faith, baptism, consecration, resurrection and the judgement to come (Hebr. vi 1, 2). Like the Thessalonians, of whom I spoke at the beginning, he had learnt to 'serve the Living GOD, and to wait for His Son from heaven, even Jesus'. He may have been taught to search the Scriptures, i.e. the sacred writings of the Jews, whether these things were so. But there is no evidence that he, or any of his contemporaries, had heard of Capernaum or Bethsaida or of what had happened there.

Of course there were still living, when Mark wrote, a few survivors of those who had been with Jesus. There was Peter himself, only recently martyred, and (as I believe) Mark had also his own

personal reminiscences of the fateful visit of Jesus
to Jerusalem. But there were now not many
surviving in Palestine, and very few indeed in the
West. They must from time to time have talked of
what they remembered, but that is a very different
thing from recording their memories in any permanent form. There has been much written in the
last few years on what is called *Formgeschichte*, much
criticism of the artificial and unsystematic way in
which Mark has strung his tales together. But this
criticism seems to me to assume that the tales
themselves had a good deal of circulation before
they were collected and turned into a narrative. Is
there any foundation for this belief? I doubt it.
The Gospel tales have left singularly few traces of
their existence apart from their incorporation into
Mark.

The view against which I am arguing is that in
the early days of Christianity, in the first century
A.D., Christianity was spread or taught by means
of tales about the career of Jesus in Galilee and
Judaea. What Mark did, as I understand the matter, was to turn the Evangel into a Biography. He
has the merits and the faults of a pioneer. It was a
discovery to find that by merely telling the tale of
the career of Jesus those who hear it said with the
Centurion 'Truly this man was a son of GOD!'
Mark compiled his tale from reminiscences of
Peter and (for the last week) from reminiscences of
his own. Others of Mark's acquaintance had no
doubt contributed their share. Some things in the

result are surely not quite historical. But so much is real reminiscence that the general outline is not far from real history.

Later writers saw that Mark could be improved. They re-edited Mark, and produced something at once more edifying and less historical. The wonder is that Mark was not simply dropped out of sight, and I think we owe the final result, viz. a co-ordinated Four, to the conservatism of the Roman Church, which was willing to accept the newer editions, but not to abandon the old original, which doubtless had first been published in Rome itself.

Let me remark in passing how few biographies exist earlier than the Gospels themselves! What book did Mark take as his model? Was he acquainted with the *Memorabilia* (ἀπομνημονεύματα) of Xenophon? Neither the language nor the style of Mark would make one think so, but it is the nearest parallel.[1]

Naturally some attempts, independent of Mark, were made to write down some of the Sayings of Jesus, for His utterances were an actual guide to the community. Even Paul records that the Lord had said that they who preach the Gospel might live by the Gospel, in other words that 'the labourer is worthy of his hire' (= Lk. x 7, Matt. x 10). Such collections may have been made in Aramaic: the famous collection now called Q appears to be a Greek translation of an Aramaic col-

[1] See Justin Martyr, 1 *Apol.* 67, *Dial.* 106.

lection of Sayings of Jesus. It is remarkable for shew-
ing a distinctly biographical, or rather personal,
interest in Jesus, for we can hardly suppose that the
famous comparison of Jesus with John the Baptist,
which tells us in passing that some of the contemporaries of Jesus thought Him too convivial to
be a messenger from GOD,[1] can have been compiled
as a catechetical manual for uninstructed converts!
No, the compiler of Q must have taken an interest
in the Sayings of Jesus for their own sake.

Further, there must have been during the first
thirty years or so after the Crucifixion some who
remembered single striking utterances of Jesus,
though they may have been quite unable to have
produced a sketch of His career. To such reminiscences I think we owe the striking but dateless
parables and tales preserved to us only in the
Gospel of Luke. We may guess that some of these
were collected at Caesarea, perhaps from the mouth
of one of the daughters of Philip, 'Apostle' or
'Evangelist', but we can know no more than that
Luke has recorded them.

It is time to return from this digression to our
proper subject, which is the collection of Sacred
Books which the Church chose as authoritative, by
which they judged the teachings and speculations
of too eager Christian thinkers. The moral is
everywhere the same: the acceptance of the annalistic as contrasted with the systematic. The Church

[1] Matt. ix 16–19, Lk. vii 31–4 ('a man gluttonous and a
winebibber').

had started with a belief which was indeed definite and systematic. It was that GOD had sent His Son to earth at this, the end of the ages, that He had died and risen again, and—that soon, very soon, in that very generation, He would return from heaven in glory to judge the world. 'They thought that the Kingdom of GOD should immediately appear.' That hope, at any rate in the form in which it was held, was not fulfilled. The wonderful thing is that Christianity itself survived. As I understand it, what is commonly known as 'Gnosticism' was a gallant effort to reformulate Christianity in terms of the current astronomy and philosophy of the day, with the Last Judgement and the Messianic Kingdom on earth left out. It failed. The Church decided still to wait, to let the old beliefs fade or survive, and meanwhile to organize itself for an extended career on this earth, and to put its trust less on constructive theories than on tradition, on the annals of what GOD had done in the past.

To us this sounds a timid and unfruitful decision, but that is because we have a vigorous faith in our modern science, our modern political theories, our modern sociology, our modern philosophy. Perhaps we are right: I do not propose to discuss such questions here. My point is that the science and the sociology of the ancient world in the Roman Empire of the second century of our era was not sound, and that a too close alliance of Christianity with that science would have proved a burden and not a bulwark. I do not think that Christianity caused the collapse of the old civilization: that collapse was, I think, inevitable. In a sense, I think the Jewish and Christian impression that the end of the ages had arrived was justified, though the old fabric took longer to collapse than they expected. Christianity survived, very well organized for a long period of decadence and twilight, for in such periods tradition, the conservation of ancient wisdom, is the safest guide.

Now we are in a new day. I do not mean 'post-War', or even since 1776: if we must name names I would rather name Copernicus and Newton. We are certainly in a new world, a world *not* the centre of the Universe; and of our Earth we know the ancient history in a way that none of the ancients, whether Jew or Gentile, knew it. In such circumstances, no doubt, we must not cling too blindly to tradition, we must reconstruct the house of our soul to fit the new conditions in which it must live. But all this is very far from the subject of these Lectures. What we have been considering is the second century of our era, and the reasons that led the Church of that day not to accept a new theology that professed to be in accordance with the spirit of that age. The Wise Man of old said there was a time for all things. That is true: the trouble is that people do not always have wisdom to know which in their time is the appropriate course. What I have been trying to shew is that when the Church of the second century rejected what seemed to be a scientific account of Religion and clung to an annalistic account it was taking a course that was appropriate to the time and therefore truly scientific.

Index

(Names of Books, e.g. *Timothy and Aquila*,
are printed in italics)

INDEX

Eschatology, 10, 18, 21, 57
Eshu Mshiha, 105, 107 f., 111
'Ethereal', 34, 49, 78, 88
Ezekiel, 128, 135
Ezra (= 'Second Esdras'), 21

Fall, the, 49 ff.
Fate, 33, 66, 88, 105
Flora, 26
'Formgeschichte', 143

Gems, 'Gnostic', 36, 83
Ginza, 101, 102, 108 f., 110 f., 113, 115
    left *G.*, 103 f., 115
Glass and wax, 76
Gnosis, 4 ff., 9, 40, 47, 57, 87, 109
'Gnostics' (sect, so-called), 58 f.
Gollancz, H., 38

Harnack, 123
Hecate, 81
Hegel, 42, 52
Hermes Trismegistos, 89, 124, 139
Hippolytus, 72, 87
Horos, 45 f., 52

Ialdabaoth (Jald-), 38, 54 f., 115
Iao, 86
Ie ie ie, 84–7
Ieu (*Jeu*), *Books of*, 39, 60, 63, 74, 83 ff.
Immortality, 33 f., 88, 125

Incarnation, Adoptionist, 72, 98 ff.
Irenaeus, *Epideixis*, 22 f., 137
    adv. Haereses, 42, 47, 50–3, 58, 80
Isaiah, Ascension of, 21

Jacopone da Todi, quoted, 18
James, M. R., 46, 122
Jeremiah, 134
Jesus, Gnostic ideas about, 39, 41, 47, 54, 66, 82
    central rôle of, 56 f., 75 ff., 88 ff.
Jewish Religion, characteristics of, 136 f.
John the Baptist, 2, 96 ff.
    Mandaean *Book of John*, 101, 111, 121
John, Revelation of, 21, 90, 123
    see also *Apocryphon of John*
Jordan, 72, 114
Journal of Theol. Studies: IV, 50 n.; XXIII, 41 n.; XXV, 42 n.; XXIX, 106 n., 108 n., 114
Justin Martyr, 93, 144

Khnub, Khnum, 39
Khuastuanift, Manichaean, 113
King, C. W., 38, 83
Knāthāyē, 102
'Knowledge of Salvation', 4, 109

INDEX

INDEX

OLD AND NEW TESTAMENTS

NEW TESTAMENT AND PISTIS SOPHIA